I0424759

NOBODY'S FOOL

How to Find Out if your Man is Cheating

By David Bishop

DISCLAIMER

The information that you are about to read is for information purposes only and does not encourage or suggest that you, the reader, take part in any activities that could be deemed illegal or unethical. In the following chapters, we will discuss in detail many investigative methods, some of them including electronic eavesdropping and recording techniques that may be a violation of privacy laws in your area. The publishers of this book do not encourage or condone any illegal activity and strongly urge you to thoroughly familiarize yourself with the applicable federal, state, and local laws. If you are uncertain as to the legality of any method that you are considering employing, you should absolutely refrain from taking any action and consult a qualified attorney for additional guidance.

NOBODY'S FOOL   How to Find Out if your Man is Cheating

© Copyright 2010

All rights reserved. This book may not be reproduced in whole or in part by any process or means without the written permission of the copyright holder.

Published by David Bishop

ISBN 1450568211
EAN 9781450568210

Table of Contents

NOBODY'S FOOL
How to Find Out if your Man is Cheating

The Purpose of This Book

To begin with, I would like to take this opportunity to commend you for taking action. I am sure that the decision to do so has not been an easy one. By seeking out and obtaining this information, you have taken a major step forward. It is the first step towards regaining control of your life. If that statement seems extreme to you, let me assure you right here and now, you have not been in control. All of that is about to change. Regaining control of your life may seem like a daunting task, but one that is worth the effort. Like all major undertakings in life, it begins with a single step forward. You have just taken that step.

Now I know what some of you are thinking right about now. You're saying to yourself that you are in control of your own life. Maybe that is what you have been telling yourself, but it is certainly not the case. It is most likely that feeling of helplessness that has led you to be reading this book.

Perhaps some of the following symptoms will sound familiar to you. If you have spent countless hours wondering about the whereabouts of your husband or boyfriend, that is not being in control. If you have spent numerous sleepless nights running through a myriad of possible scenarios in your mind, that is not being in control. Do you find yourself questioning your own sensibilities, and wondering if you are simply becoming overly paranoid? Do you find yourself distracted and unable to focus at work? Do any of the above situations sound familiar to you? Most likely they do. These are all signs that you are no longer in control, but rather the circumstances around you are controlling your life.

You may have found that the stress of not knowing what is happening in your own relationship has manifested itself in some form of physical ailment. Headaches, stomach upset, high blood pressure, irritability, loss of appetite, insomnia, and anxiety attacks are only of few of the many symptoms of stress. Side effects such as these can range from being mildly unpleasant to serious medical conditions. I should, at this time, mention that if you are experiencing any conditions similar to those mentioned above, you should seek the advice of a qualified medical professional. I cannot cure your physical ailments, but together, we *can* attack the cause of them.

So the purpose of this book is very simple and straightforward. The purpose of this book is to find answers to your questions and seek out the truth. And it is said; "The truth will set you free". Before we address the many questions that you have, there is one question that I must ask of you. There is an old saying that states "if you are going to ask a question, you better be sure that you want the answer". So I ask of you now, before we go any further, are you sure you want the answers that we are about to seek out? It is my belief that you have already asked and answered that question for yourself. That said, I would be remiss if I did not ask it one last time.

Most people, in fact, will go through a long period of uncertainty before taking the action that you have taken today. It is not uncommon for many weeks or even months of suspicion to precede the realization that something is wrong. Often times a person will think that their suspicions are the result of an over active imagination or simple paranoia. Similar to the five stages of the grieving process, the first stage in confronting the possibility of an unfaithful partner is denial. I think by this point, you have come to realize that burying your head in the sand and ignoring your fears has not improved the situation, nor has it made you feel any better. Even if your fears turn out to be unfounded, I am sure you have noticed that they are having an adverse affect on your relationship. For that reason, I am of the opinion that the only logical choice is to seek out and uncover the truth. There simply comes a point when getting answers to your questions becomes the only way to move forward.

In this text, I will share with you some very simple, as well as some more advanced techniques to gather information and get the answers to those questions. Many of these techniques are the same ones used by professional investigators, while conducting marital investigations. Those same private detectives probably would rather I kept this information to myself. The investigative industry is extremely lucrative, and a good private investigator can make a substantial living specializing in marital and fidelity type investigations. Most will charge in the range of $50-$100 per hour, and approximately $400-$700 per day for surveillance. Now I am not knocking the investigative industry by any means. Most Private Detectives are highly skilled professionals who offer a valuable service in return for their fee. I am simply offering you an easier and more cost effective approach to your investigative needs.

In the following pages, you will learn about some of the telltale signs of infidelity. These signs will give you a good indication as to whether or not your suspicions are justified. From that point, you will learn how to document your partner's actions and movements to determine if there is a pattern of suspicious behavior. Finally, I will show you how to collect conclusive proof of a person's infidelity.

For some of you, the conclusion of this process will bring great relief, as you discover that your significant other has not been unfaithful at all and that your suspicions have been unwarranted. For others, the end result may hold much more unpleasant news, perhaps with devastating consequences. Either way, you will be able to bring this period of fear and uncertainty to an ultimate conclusion. One way or another, you will be able to move on with your life.

Regardless of the outcome of your investigative efforts, what you do with the information you obtain is none of my business. Nor is it the business of anyone else. Each person must make their own choices in life, and ultimately live with the repercussions of those choices. If you come to find that your spouse or partner has not been untrue, you will achieve the peace of mind that we all deserve, and be able to move on with your life. You will have found the answers to those nagging questions, and you will have done so without the embarrassment or consequences of confronting him with a battery of false accusations.

If, however, the end result of your actions is the realization that your mate has been unfaithful, only you can decide what course of action you take next. If you choose to confront your partner with your findings, you will be able to do so based on documented facts and not wild speculation or inaccurate assumptions. You may seek out counseling in an attempt to repair the damage done by the affair, or you may find that the wounds of infidelity are too deep, and that your relationship has ultimately suffered irreparable harm. Again, those types of decisions are ones that only you can make.

If the incidence of infidelity occurs within a legal or even a common-law marriage, you may find yourself contemplating a legal separation or divorce. If that should be the case, you will be able to use the information you have gathered in any subsequent court proceeding. Additionally, the documentation of your spouse's illicit activities could become a powerful bargaining chip when negotiating a divorce or property settlement agreement. Keep in mind that without such documentation, you will not be able to substantiate any of your claims of infidelity. Your spouse could potentially turn the tables by filing for divorce and making outrageous claims about you. I have seen this happen countless times. Without proof or at least documentation of your partner's actions, the proceedings could come down to a simple case of "he said, she said".

So I write this book with one simple purpose in mind, and that is to help you to find the answers that you so desperately seek. What you do from that point on is a subject for a later date. I am no marriage counselor and am not qualified to advise you on how to proceed. I am no Dr. Phil, nor am I Dr. Ruth or Jerry Springer. I cannot hold your hand, anymore than I can offer you a shoulder to cry on. I apologize if this sounds cold or uncaring. In fact, I care deeply about people and wish you the best. Over the years I have come to the conclusion that the best way that I can help you, is to provide you with the skills and the techniques to allow you to take back control of your life. With that said, let's turn the page and begin.

What Is Cheating?

Cheating, it certainly is nothing new. Throughout the ages, dating back to our earliest written texts, there have been accounts of infidelity. Books, films, television programs, everywhere we look, it seems, there are references to people being unfaithful to one another. It's been called many things; unfaithfulness, cheating, stepping out. But at what point has a person actually crossed the line? What constitutes cheating?

To put it simply, there is no definitive answer. The answer is different for everyone. The distance between Bill Clinton's opinion on the matter and Mother Theresa's, would needless to say, be substantial. I think it's safe to assume, that you and I, as well as most people, fall somewhere in the middle. We've all heard the funny little expressions, the sayings that refer to being faithful. "Look, don't touch" or "You can look at the menu, but you just can't order anything". But let's take a more technical view.

One of the definitions of *cheating* listed in Webster's New Collegiate Dictionary is "to be sexually unfaithful". That definition seems rather narrow though, don't you think? I prefer Webster's definition of *infidelity*, which states "marital unfaithfulness or an instance of it" or "unfaithfulness to a moral obligation: disloyalty".

Regardless of what is or isn't cheating, it can take a variety of forms. Most people associate infidelity with a physical interaction between two people. Put simply, sex. But is the act of engaging in sexual intercourse the only type of cheating? I think not. Infidelity takes place on many different levels, not just the physical. There is also a mental and emotional component to infidelity. Whether it be in film or in reality, we have all heard a confronted cheater say "it didn't mean anything" or "she means nothing to me". Does that somehow mean that the act of sex was any less an act of disloyalty? What about the married man who loves another, but has never had physical contact with her? Has he been unfaithful? On an emotional level, perhaps yes.

One thing that you should keep in mind is that one type of illicit behavior can, often times, just be the beginning. Many cheaters will "test the waters" by experimenting on the Internet. If your partner is involved in some less serious form of activity, the situation will often escalate. I sometimes think of chat rooms as the gateway drug of infidelity. As cliché as it may sound, one thing, often does, lead to another.

To make the subject even more confusing than it already is, one must keep in mind that there are certain cultural aspects to infidelity. In some foreign cultures, men having mistresses is considered not only to be completely acceptable, but in some cases, a status symbol. Now, I'm sure you are thinking of some far off land or of a turban-topped sheik brooding over his harem, but we don't have to look that far. Let's not forget our polygamist friends, such as those in Utah, living right here in our country. For them, having multiple wives is not only considered their right, but actually God's will. Age can also have a significant impact on a person's views of infidelity. Our younger generations tend to have a more casual point of view regarding relationships, commitment, and sometimes sex.

In today's age of the Internet and the World Wide Web, a whole new realm of opportunity has been created for the would-be cheater. You don't have to surf the Internet for very long to stumble across the many opportunities to meet and interact with people in a virtual environment. Chat rooms, instant messengers, an online dating websites make cheating easier than ever. Some websites even specialize in helping married or otherwise attached individuals to find partners for clandestine affairs. We'll discuss how to track and catch a cheater on the Internet in later chapters.

For married couples, the terms of the contract between both parties seems to be more black and white. After all, just about every wedding ceremony involves the reciting of marital vows. To love, honor and cherish. That seems pretty cut and dry doesn't it? As for honor, that is a pretty broad term, but I think we all have a pretty good idea of what it means to abide by your wedding vows.

Obviously, you don't have to be married to be involved in a committed relationship. For unmarried couples, certain expectations and boundaries still exist. Some couples will have open discussions about what they expect from each other. Others have not had such explicit conversations, but that does not mean a commitment does not exist. The level of commitment, and the understanding between two people is what will ultimately define what is and is not acceptable behavior. There is a certain bond, or trust, that exists within all relationships. Whether or not that bond is implied or implicit, is inconsequential.

I have heard countless explanations of what is considered acceptable within a relationship. They have ranged from one extreme to the other. As I mentioned earlier, some people feel that sex is a necessary element of cheating. I have heard others say that looking at another person is cheating. One person once told me that they did not believe that a one-night stand should be considered being unfaithful, and that only an ongoing affair was an act of infidelity.

As you can see, there are many opinions about what constitutes cheating. Quite frankly, there is nothing wrong with that. What is a problem is when two people who are in a relationship with each other, have dissimilar viewpoints on the subject. Obviously, that will become a problem at some point in their relationship. Often times, the problem lies with a difference of personalities rather than a difference of opinions. If one person is extremely outgoing and a *people person*, while their partner is shy and introverted, that in and of itself could cause a great deal of misunderstanding. Some people are what we call *touchy-feely*, and seem to be constantly hugging people. That may be completely normal behavior to the hugger, but be completely unacceptable behavior in the eyes of his or her partner. Now let me be perfectly clear here, I have nothing against people who hug, but there is a big difference between hugging and groping.

So what is cheating? I've tried to give you a little commentary on the topic, as well as some food for thought. If you feel that you have been betrayed, or that there has been a violation of your trust, in my humble opinion, that constitutes unfaithfulness. In the end, it is a question that only you can answer. And don't let anyone tell you otherwise.

Where There's Smoke,
There's Fire. (Or is there?)

So the question before us remains; is he or isn't he? Let's start out by putting things into perspective. If you have come to the point that you have sought out this information, you have obviously been having some very serious reservations about the fidelity of your mate. Now don't get me wrong, everyone has the right to be a little jealous once in awhile. But we are not talking about a little jealousy here. We are talking about an ongoing and sustained level of suspicion. In a court of law, a jury is instructed that there must be a *preponderance of evidence* to prove guilt. Although this is not a legal proceeding, and your partner will not likely be tried for his actions, this is still a good guideline to follow. In other words, if you notice one or two instances of unusual behavior, there may be a perfectly simple and innocent explanation behind it. If you do, however, begin to notice multiple instances of unusual behavior, you would be justified to become suspicious.

Before we shine a spotlight on your partner, perhaps this would be a good time to take a good look at yourself and your own psyche. You must look at your own personality as well as the way you interact with your partner, not only in the present, but also in the past. We must consider the way in which you interact with your current partner, as well as past partners. There are a few simple questions that you should ask yourself and try to answer as honestly as possible.

- ❑ Do you consider yourself a jealous person?
- ❑ Do you consider yourself paranoid?
- ❑ Has a previous partner ever cheated on you in the past?
- ❑ Was the infidelity ever substantiated? (Proven)
- ❑ Have you ever made accusations against a past or present partner that turned out to be false?

If you answered yes to more than two of the above questions, I would advise you to proceed with caution. If you did answer yes to more than two of the above questions, that does not necessarily mean that your suspicions are not warranted. I only suggest that you proceed slowly.

Now let's focus the attention on your partner, and the ways in which he interacts with you. There is a history to every relationship, and within that history can be numerous clues.

- ❑ When you first began dating your current partner, was he seeing someone else? Were you the other woman?
- ❑ Has your partner ever told you that he had cheated on someone else?
- ❑ Has your current partner ever cheated on you in the past?
- ❑ Was the infidelity ever substantiated? (Proven)
- ❑ Was there more than one instance of infidelity?

If you answered yes to more than two of the above questions, you may have reason for concern. It is often said "once a cheat, always a cheat". If your partner has a history of infidelity, the odds that he is being unfaithful to you are elevated. If your partner has cheated on every other person that he has ever been involved with, don't kid yourself, he will cheat on you.

Even if you are not aware of any past history of your partner being disloyal, we should examine the overall character of your mate. A person's level of honesty and integrity will often be apparent throughout many aspects of their life.

- ❏ Would you characterize your partner as "dishonest"?
- ❏ Have you ever heard your partner lie to someone else?
- ❏ Have you ever caught your partner in a lie about something?
- ❏ Has your partner ever stolen something from you or someone else?
- ❏ Would your partner cheat while playing a game? (Board games, cards, sports, etc.)
- ❏ If a clerk gave your partner too much change after a purchase, would he keep it or return it?

If you answered yes to more than two of the above questions, you may have reason for concern. In my experience, most dishonest people will lie about some things and not about others. They will, however, be *willing* to lie about anything. Once a liar, always a liar. If he has lied to others, he will be willing to lie to you. Even if his other instances of dishonesty have nothing to do with fidelity, it still demonstrates a lack of integrity. That is a key component of all cheaters.

One other telling sign of a person's morality is how he views dishonest behavior by others. We have all had times where we discover a friend or a family member has either cheated on their mate, or been cheated on. What was your mate's view of the infidel? Did he defend the cheater? Did he make comments like "the way she nags at him, I'm not surprised"? Or perhaps, he said nothing at all. This alone can be a telling sign. Try this test. The next time that you and your mate are in a group setting, say with some friends, you can bring up an imaginary coworker who just found out that her husband has been having an affair. Watch how your partner reacts to the conversation. Maybe he will avoid eye contact during the conversation, or perhaps his face will become a bit flushed. You may see him squirm in his seat a little. These are all signs that he is uncomfortable with the topic, and probably feeling guilt as he listens to others chastise the cheater.

As we are beginning to examine what makes your partner tick, we should keep in mind that your own view may be biased. You should always try to listen intently to what others have to say about your partner. Now remember, some of those people may have a biased view of your mate as well. Some may love him, and some may hate him, but at least their opinions are from a different perspective than your own. Keep in mind the above questions about your partner.

❑ Would your friends have answered those questions favorably?
❑ Would his friends have answered those questions favorably?
❑ Have your friends ever made accusations about your partner?

❑ Have you ever had to defend your partner to your friends?

❑ Have your friends ever told you specifically that they think your partner is untrustworthy?

In this case, any yes answers should be reason for concern. If you answered yes to three or more of the above questions, you should be re-examining your own view of your partner.

Another question that many people ask is; why do cheaters cheat? For the purposes of this text, that question may not seem relevant. The motives behind infidelity do not make a person any more or less guilty of the offense. If we understand some of the reasons why people cheat, however, it may give us some insight into whether or not our partner is being unfaithful. By examining this, we can begin to see if the person in question fits a particular profile.

❑ *The Habitual or Serial Cheater.* This is the stereotypical person who just does not seem to be capable of being faithful to anyone. His past will be checkered with a long list of failed relationships and instances of infidelity. Characteristics of this type of cheater would be that he has always been viewed as a flirt and a player.

❑ *The Opportunistic Cheater.* This person is not constantly looking to engage in extracurricular activities as the habitual cheater is, but is open to the idea if the circumstances should present themselves. Because he is not actively pursuing other partners, long periods of time may pass without any instance of infidelity. Characteristics of the opportunistic cheater are an overall lack of moral character and integrity. Someone who is easily swayed.

- ❑ ***The Unhappy Cheater.*** This type of person will swear up and down that they are not the unfaithful type, but have simply been driven to infidelity by an unhappy marriage or relationship. Characteristics of this cheater would be one that always seems to think that their lot in life is someone else's fault. The *poor me* type.

- ❑ ***The Center of Attention Cheater.*** This person craves attention of all kinds. Not only attention from members of the opposite sex, but from all people. He will always try to be the life of the party, and will often times be a good joke teller. He will be charming and personable, and sometimes quite a flirt. Characteristics of this type of cheater will be that he seems to be a completely different person when alone with his mate than when with a group of people. Friends and family will often react in disbelief when told of this type of person's negative side.

All cheaters, no matter how careful, will leave clues of their activities. Now I am not talking about forensic evidence here, and we're not going to go in search of any DNA samples. I'm talking about clues that will be much easier to spot. Attitudes, habits, patterns and statements are all clues that will begin to become increasingly apparent. Many cheaters will leave clues behind on purpose. Some actually have a strong subconscious desire to be caught. Others will flaunt their behavior in an attempt to provoke or harm their partner. If your partner is insecure and the jealous type, he may be trying to bring about similar feelings in you. This type of person will do this in retaliation for behavior that has made him to feel jealous, regardless of whether that behavior was a real or imagined.

Once you start looking for them, the clues of infidelity will become increasingly visible. Obviously, you have already spotted some type of clues or you wouldn't be suspicious in the first place. You already have a heightened level of awareness, but you need to become even more aware. Most of all, we are looking for a change in pattern. Activities that seem out of the ordinary or a break in routine.

Once you start to take notice of behavior that you believe is suspicious, most times you will begin to see a pattern forming. You must begin to document your partner's activities. I suggest that you use a journal or notebook to log critical information. Take note of his comings and goings, as well as incoming and outgoing phone calls. Be sure to include dates, times and circumstances as well as explanations given by your mate. Make sure to note the day of the week. If your mate does not work a typical 9-to-5, Monday through Friday job, you will also want to note his work schedule on the day in question.

You should also be aware of times that your partner spends on the computer. Remember, if a person is communicating with someone by way of Instant Messenger or a chat room on the Internet, they will often have a pre-set time designated to "meet". Make notes of any other suspicious occurrences. It may not seem important at the time, but may be critical at a later date when you are trying to piece together his whereabouts. As time goes on, you may begin to see patterns forming. This will assist you in not only ascertaining if your partner is cheating, but also will give you clues as to where and when to look for evidence. You may begin to notice patterns as to days of the week, or time of day, when your partner's whereabouts are unaccounted for. For example: you may notice that he seems to work late every other Tuesday, or that he has unexpected business obligations every month on the 10th. Take thorough notes and include anything that you even remotely feel could be important. Start recording information immediately, today. Of course, you should keep this journal in a safe place where you are certain that your mate will not come across it, either accidentally or otherwise.

As you begin to gather information, try to remain calm and patient. I know that is not easy to do. You should try to be objective and unbiased in your observations, but I know that is a near impossible task to accomplish. Do the best you can. Most importantly, you must trust your gut and go from there. Do not try to rationalize your partner's actions. You have instincts, use them. You do not need anyone else, to validate your feelings. You are not losing your mind or becoming a paranoid schizophrenic.

Most of all, remember that cheating is always the cheaters fault, not yours. You must trust in the belief that you will have the final say in the matter, but you must wait until you have found undeniable proof of infidelity before taking any further steps. If a cheater suspects that you are onto him, he will most likely become more careful about his activities or may even temporarily suspend the affair until he feels that you have let your guard down again. He may even try to do things to appease you or to lull you back into a state of complacency, so it is imperative that you not let on that you suspect him. As difficult as it may seem, you must make every effort to remain patient and act as natural as possible. It may be very difficult to resist the urge to confront him, but resist you must. The time for confrontation and to expose your partner will come in due time, but it must come at a time and place of your choosing.

Case Study

Jenny & Tom

Jenny and Tom had been dating for over eight years, and by all accounts had been through thick and thin together. With her 30th birthday rapidly approaching, Jenny was becoming more and more inpatient and desperately wanted an engagement ring. She loved Tom very much, but understood that marriage would be easier when they were both more established in their careers and after Jenny finished her schooling as a dental hygienist. When she spoke to her friends about Tom and their relationship together, she would always make references to the future with absolute certainty that the two would someday be married and live the rest of their lives *happily ever after*. She would often begin statements with the phrase "after Tom and I get married...". She never doubted for a moment that they would always be together.

Tom was an assistant manager for a popular restaurant chain and had been with the company for several years. He started as a cook and worked his way up to kitchen manager before entering the company's management training program. Tom's career was going well and he was in line to get his own restaurant from the chain in a few years. There was one glaring difference between Jenny and Tom that was quite apparent to their friends whenever they got together. Although Jenny was always quick to talk about marriage and would drop the "M" word at numerous times throughout the conversation, Tom would never mention anything about the prospect of marriage or any permanency to their relationship.

Although a bit stocky, Tom was a charismatic guy and moderately good looking. He loved to kid around with his coworkers and never had trouble making friends. Over the years there had been times when accusations were made about Tom's wandering eye. After all, a bustling restaurant with a lively bar crowd can be a great place to work if a guy wants to meet women. There is a pretty high turnover rate within the restaurant industry, so there was always a new crop of waitresses and hostesses coming through the doors. At one point, a sexual-harassment complaint was filed by an underage employee, alleging that Tom had gotten "fresh" with her. The news didn't come as much of a surprise to the people who knew him. Over the years, Tom had developed quite a reputation as a flirt.

There were even a several times that some of Jenny's good friends approached her and told her that Tom had made advances on them or that they were aware of his inappropriate behavior. Jenny always vehemently defended Tom claiming that he would never, ever do *something like that.* Over time, the friends who had made such accusations seemed to disappear from Jenny's life. The remaining friends knew never to question Tom's fidelity, as it would certainly result in the end of their friendship.

Eventually, Tom was caught in the act at a local tavern, sharing and after work cocktail with a coworker. He was getting rather friendly with the young girl when

Jenny unexpectedly walked in. Jenny was of course devastated and swiftly ended the relationship.

In the weeks that followed, like most jilted girlfriends, she spent a great deal of time being consoled by her friends. They were all supportive and really felt bad for Jenny. During this time, Jenny began to realize that none of her friends seemed the least bit surprised by this shocking turn of events. After considerable prodding, they all admitted that they were well aware of Tom's disloyal tendencies and that they had been for quite some time. Some of them had first-hand knowledge and had seen Tom around town with other women. Others had just heard stories secondhand, about his philandering. In the end, they all said the same thing; that they were afraid to say anything to Jenny, for fear that she would turn on them and defend Tom. Jenny was even more distraught after her friends' revelations and simply could not believe that they would not have told her what was going on.

I always advise people to trust their gut intuition and follow their own instincts. That does not mean that you should not take into account the things that the people around you are saying about your partner. You should always consider the source. If someone that you know well and trust is suspicious of him, you would be well advised to at least consider what they have to say. Jenny buried her head in the sand and ignored the countless signs that Tom was being unfaithful. She also refused to hear what the people close to her were saying. Although her friends meant well and had Jenny's best interest at heart, she simply did not want to hear what they had to say.

100 Telltale Signs
That He Is Cheating

Most books will include an index and/or glossary at the conclusion of the text. Although that is the customary location for such information, I have decided to do something a little different by including this section here. On the pages that follow, I have created a list of over 100 of the most common signs that your partner is cheating. The list is by no means all-inclusive, but it does cover a large majority of the potential circumstances that you need to be on the lookout for.

Now remember, some of these signs will apply to even the most faithful of husbands or partners. There can be reasonable and completely innocent explanations for many of them. What we are looking for is multiple signs. So read through the following pages carefully. You should look for anything that sounds familiar, or has happened in the past. Additionally, it will give you an extensive list of things to look out for from this point forward. A bell might go off in your head after reading some of these telltale signs, as you realize that your partner is beginning to fit the profile. If you own this text, you can make notations in the margins next to each entry as to whether or not the corresponding sign is apparent in your relationship.

Absences   Any unaccounted absences should be reason for concern. Within a healthy relationship, it is rare for either party to be unaware of their partner's whereabouts.   You should also be aware of vague or uncomfortable explanations regarding the absence.

Activities   New activities or hobbies in and of themselves are not reason for concern, but coupled with other signs, it can be an indicator.   Especially if the activity takes him away from the home on a regular basis.   The activity may be a cover to account for his absence.

Alcohol   Increased alcohol consumption, either at home or elsewhere, can be reason for concern.   The drinking can be a result of guilt or anxiety, or can be a part of his social activities.   Be aware of signs of impairment or the odor of liquor when he returns home.

Anxiety   Increased levels of anxiety can have a variety of causes, including work and financial pressures.   It can also be the result of guilt or the fear of being caught.

Appearance   Be aware of any changes in his overall appearance.   Appearance is a broad term, and everyone has the right to make changes on occasion.   Watch for drastic changes and those that appear out of character.   Often times, cheaters will try to freshen up their look and appear younger than their age.

ATM machines   As with any social relationship, carrying on a clandestine affair can cost money.   Take note of any additional cash being drawn from your bank accounts. ATM receipts will show amounts of withdrawals, as well as date, time, and location of the transaction.

Attitude A sudden change of attitude is certainly cause for concern. Most importantly, be aware of his attitude towards you. He may be disrespectful and seem disinterested in the details of your day. His attitude may also change regarding work, kids, home life, etc.

Bank accounts Be aware of changes in your checking and savings accounts. Watch for unusual deposits and withdrawals on your monthly statement.

Bars There are many happily married men *and* women who spend time in bars, pubs or taverns. Some men go out for a drink with their friends after work, or watch a game at a sports bar. If this is the norm within your relationship, that is fine. But if your partner has only recently begun spending time in bars, this may be a cause for concern.

Bed Any change in pattern regarding the bedroom, or the bed in particular, should be noted. If you suspect that your partner is having a sexual relationship in his home, or your's if you share a common home, be aware of the bed sheets, pillows, and blankets. Evidence of sex on the sheets or make up on the pillowcases are all incriminating pieces of evidence. The cheater may have a new interest in laundering the bedding in an effort to conceal evidence. Keep in mind; the mattress or mattress pad may still have signs of illicit activity, such as the smell of perfume, even if the sheets have been freshly laundered.

Behavior   As with attitude, the key to spotting telling behavior is by simply looking for a change.   The behavior does not necessarily need to be better *or* worse, just different.

Body image   Everyone, regardless of their age or relationship status, is aware of their body image. The longer you spend in a relationship, the more relaxed you tend to become about your body image. Body image issues become magnified when faced with the prospect of disrobing in front of someone for the first time. If your partner seems to be spending more time in front of the full-length mirror, or asking your opinion about his physique, this may be a warning sign.

Breath   Everyone knows the feeling of unexpectedly running into a friend or acquaintance right after consuming a meal laced with garlic at your favorite Italian restaurant. A cheater will be more aware of his breath.   You may see him, brushing his teeth more often, especially before going out, or avoiding pungent foods all together.

Business cards   We all collect business cards of people that we meet and interact with in our everyday life. Take note of any business cards you come across, especially those of women and of businesses and occupations that don't seem to fit your partner's line of work or interests.

Caller ID   Just about everyone has this feature on their home phone these days. It displays the phone number, and in some cases the name of the incoming caller. Keep an eye out for unfamiliar names and numbers, especially those that were received when you were out of the house and your partner was home alone.

Everyone receives, wrong number calls occasionally, but take note of an unfamiliar number calling on numerous occasions.

Car   Your partner's automobile can many times be the scene of the crime. If you share a car, it will be easier to make observations. If you don't, you'll have to find opportunities to inspect the inside of the vehicle without his knowledge. Look for any incriminating items that may have been left behind by your partner or the other woman. Check to see if the ashtray has been used if your partner is a non-smoker. Take notice of the position of both the driver and passenger seats.

Cards   Greeting cards have distinct envelopes and can be easily spotted in a bundle of mail, even if you don't get a chance to take a close look at. Check the return address of any mysterious cards, as well as the postmark from where it was sent.

Cell phones   The popularity of cellular phones has created a new and more clandestine way for a cheater to communicate with the other woman. Be aware of excessive cell phone usage. If you have access to his cell phone, you can review the log of the incoming and outgoing phone calls, as well as the dates and times of those phone calls. This information can be cross-referenced with your journal entries.

Chat room   Internet chat rooms have become a common way that people can meet and communicate with one another on a somewhat anonymous basis. If an adult is spending an excessive amount of time in a chat room, he may be seeking out potential partners. Many chat rooms will have a theme. Therefore, you should be on the lookout for chat rooms that cater to singles or have any type of sexual theme.

Checkbooks   Today's increasingly paperless society has made the use of actual paper checks more and more of a rarity.   The checkbook register, however, should not be overlooked as a source of information.   Keep in mind that many people will enter ATM or check card purchases in their checkbook register.   As always, keep an eye out for anything that seems out of the ordinary.

Chores   Most women would not object to their boyfriend or husband doing additional chores around the house.   This on its own would not be considered to be suspicious activity.   The motive for taking on additional chores however, may be reason to have a closer look.   Many unfaithful husbands will do additional chores around the house simply out of guilt, or to keep their partner from nagging about other suspicious activity.   Doing these extra chores, immediately following an unexplained absence would certainly fit the bill.

Clothing   Any change in your partner's attire is worth noting, especially if the change is for the better.   Men who are involved in a committed relationship will often become complacent about their appearance and the way that they dress.   If he suddenly takes an interest in purchasing new clothing, take note.   Be aware of changes in how he dresses for work.   He may just be bucking for a promotion but he might be trying to impress someone other than his boss.

Cologne   A change of scent is one that is easily detectable.   Men are well aware that women love a man who smells good.   If your man does not usually wear cologne, and suddenly does, there is a reason behind it. He may already wear cologne but make a change to something new and trendy.

Communication It is said that communication is the key to every relationship. You can tell a great deal about a couple by what they say, and don't say to one another. There are patterns of communication that exist within every relationship as well. Look for changes in those patterns. He may begin to use new expressions or phrases that you have not heard him use before. Just like he picked up patterns of speech from you when you first began to date, he may be doing the same with another partner. Also, be aware if he becomes considerably more quiet and distant than usual.

Commuting The way in which your partner travels to and from work can be a key in ascertaining when and where he is meeting with another woman. If he takes mass transportation to work, but begins to take the car on Tuesdays, that begs the question; where else is he going during his commute to and from work, as well as during his lunch hour. Be aware of earlier departure times as well as late arrivals. There is no set rule that says that infidelity only takes place during the evening hours.

Comparisons No one likes to be compared to someone else. If that type of behavior is taking place in addition to other warning signs, you should be especially aware. Although he may claim that the comparisons are to a family member or other innocent party, he may in fact be comparing you to the other woman.

Computer As I have mentioned earlier, the computer holds countless opportunities for people to meet and communicate with one another. If your partner seems to be spending an excessive amount of time on the computer, or if he seems to be more secretive about his computer usage, you should take note. You may notice that he tends to use the computer only while you are in the shower or after you have gone to bed. If he uses a laptop computer, he may close it to obscure the screen when you approach. Additionally, if he moves the computer from one part of the home to another to afford more privacy, this is definitely a danger sign.

Confidence Generally, this is viewed as a positive character trait, but again, we are looking for deviations from the norm. If your partner seems to be more confident, and even more full of himself than usual, it may be the result of a recent conquest of some sort.

Coworkers He may have mentioned someone that he works with. It may be someone new in the office. Remember that the workplace is a highly convenient location to initiate an affair. If he has an interest in someone at work, you may find that the name comes up often. This may be a result of his thoughts being preoccupied by the other woman.

Credit cards In the paperless society, plastic is king. Credit cards have become the number one method of purchase in the United States. This of course includes cheating related expenditures, as well as legitimate purchases. Many purchases can only be made by way of a credit card. Purchases made over the phone or the Internet are examples of that very fact. Hotels will usually require a credit card to secure a room. The great thing about credit cards is that they leave a clear and easy to follow trail. You can look at the cheaters credit card history, by way of his monthly statement.

Many cards also offer online access to a credit card account. If you have the opportunity to physically look at the card, you'll find a toll-free number on the back. Please be aware that accessing someone else's credit card information may be illegal. If you are married, perhaps the account is held jointly. Either way, you would most likely need a password or the last four digits of the account holder's social security number to obtain information.

Criticism   If you find that your partner has become overly critical of you, keep in mind that he may be making comparisons to someone else. Criticism, ugly as it may be, is a prevalent part of many relationships. What we are looking for here is an elevated level of critical behavior.

Defensiveness   When a cheater is confronted or questioned by his partner, he may display defensive behavior. This type of response will usually seem to be somewhat child-like and an over-reaction to your inquiry.

Diet   You may notice that your partner has changed his eating habits on a day to day basis. Often times, a cheater will become more conscious of his weight at the onset of a romantic relationship. Obviously, he may just be finally trying to take care of himself better after years of neglect.

Dining out   When people tell a lie, there will often be elements of truth within the lie. It is much easier for the brain to process a partial lie rather than a completely fictitious account. It is also easier to remember and recite a story when only one or two elements are less than accurate. A cheater will often claim to have dinner plans with a friend or coworker, when he is really dining out with the other woman. This also makes it easier to account for other related details such as credit card expenditures, or his car being seen at the restaurant.

Dinner Dinnertime in many households is considered to be a very important element of family life. It is often the only time of the day when the family gathers together and discusses each other's daily activities. Your partner, and specifically husbands and fathers, may avoid family dinner, as it is a catalyst of feelings of guilt. He may be more frequently having dinner at work or after work, with a coworker.

Drive-bys Infidelity can often mirror the behavior of high school age teens, much more so than that of mature adults. Illicit relationships will many times have a very immature element to them. What most women do not realize is that the other woman will likely be just as jealous of you, as you are of her. If you notice a car driving slowly past your home, especially in the evening, take note of the vehicle and of the driver. Be extra aware if you begin to see the same vehicle numerous times.

Drugs Certainly drugs on their own are an extremely dangerous problem for any relationship. I think that goes without saying. But for purposes of this book, a change or increase in drug usage may be a sign of additional problems. Sometimes drug use will be something that the two parties have in common. If your husband smoked marijuana in college, but has not used it in over 10 years, I would be suspicious if he suddenly began to use again. Additionally, I would question where someone who has not been actively involved in the drug culture would have bought or acquired the marijuana.

Eating habits   You may notice different attitudes regarding food from your partner, some of which can be associated with their weight as mentioned under Diet. You may also notice changes in appetite or preferences, which can have a wide range of causes.   Guilt can drastically affect a person's appetite, for one thing.   Or you may notice that your partner seems to be more adventurous when it comes to trying different types of foods.   Affairs often involve experimenting and trying new things on many levels.   If he should mention in passing that he loves Thai food, but you have never been to a Thai restaurant together, you would of course be justified in becoming suspicious.

E-mail   This has become an extremely popular way to communicate.   If you have access to your partner's computer, you may be able to read e-mails that he has sent as well as received.   If he is being unfaithful and knows that you have access to the computer, he would more than likely be careful to delete any incriminating e-mails.   Some programs will allow you to view recently deleted mail.   You may also be able to explore the PCs "filing cabinet" to find evidence of suspicious correspondence.   Also, be sure to check the address book for names of contacts that you are unfamiliar with.

Errands   You may find that your partner suddenly seems more in enthusiastic about running to the store or to the dry cleaner.   If he only seems eager about going to specific stores or locations, I would begin to wonder if he has interest in someone who works there.   If he does not usually run household errands and has only begun to do so lately, it may also be a sign of guilt or of trying to keep you from questioning or nagging about his activities.

Exercise   Some men take a renewed interest in physical fitness as they realize they are getting older and are not in as good a shape as they once were. This can be completely normal and not be a subject for concern. If his newfound exercise regimen is coupled with other signs mentioned here, I would definitely take notice.

Favors   Has your husband or boyfriend been offering to do favors for you more often lately? This falls under the same category as errands, and chores. He may be trying to keep you happy, which will in turn keep your guard down.

Flowers   Traditionally, flowers given from a man to a woman are a sign of affection, and are often associated with the courtship process. Any receipts or charges that appear on a credit card statement for a florist should be questioned. Of course, you should wait a reasonable amount of time to ensure that the flowers are not for you. If you have been suspicious, and suddenly find yourself in receipt of a lovely bouquet from your partner, you should consider that this might also be a sign of guilt or appeasement.

Freudian slips   We have all heard the term, but do you know what it really means? A Freudian slip is when someone accidentally reveals information that they did not consciously want to divulge.   This happens constantly, and under many circumstances. Sometimes it seems that the more you try to keep information secret, the more likely you are to slip up and say the wrong thing.

Gifts (given) You are certainly justified and warranted in being suspicious if you find that your significant other has been giving gifts to other women. Remember, gifts do not need to be the typical romantic gestures that we expect, such as flowers, candy or jewelry. A thoughtful gift can be anything, but of course extra attention should be paid to gifts of a more intimate nature. Gifts, like any purchase, will leave a paper trail behind.

Gifts (received) If your partner has *received* presents from another woman, that would also be cause for serious concern. You may notice him wearing a new article of clothing such as a tie, or he may be wearing a new piece of jewelry. If he commonly makes these types of purchases for himself, it should not be a reason to suspect. Keep in mind that women will often buy items for men that a man would not commonly purchase for himself. Simply put, women have different tastes than men, and you can often spot a gift that was given by a woman as opposed to something that was purchased by the man himself.

Glasses If your partner requires spectacles in order to see, he may feel insecure about wearing his glasses around a new love interest. He may decide to switch from his glasses to contact lenses, or even consider surgery such as LASIK in order to eliminate the need for eyewear. This is a common sign that he is more concerned about his appearance and has a desire to look more youthful.

Grooming This is a broad term and can apply to the many ways people tend to their own appearance. Haircuts, shaving and manicures are all things that men do to try to look neat and appealing to members of the opposite sex. As men get older, they often have to deal with hair growing in places that it previously did not. Extra attention to trimming nose and ear hair may become apparent. Trimming of pubic hair may also be a sign that he anticipates that someone new will be seeing him without his clothes on.

Guilt   As mentioned previously on numerous occasions, many cheaters will feel tremendous guilt for their unfaithfulness. This can manifest itself in a variety of behaviors as well as physical side effects. Sometimes a guilty conscience can be the hardest piece of evidence to conceal.

Gym   Increasing one's activity level by way of physical exercise is also a sign that your man is thinking more about his physical appearance than he has in the past. By joining and frequenting a gym, he is not only getting in shape and making himself potentially more appealing to other women, but he is also in a very social setting with considerable opportunities to make new acquaintances.

Hair   A fresh new haircut or a new, more modern hairstyle can be a nice change for anyone. As with other signs, it can be an indicator that your partner is beginning to take more interest in his physical appearance. These changes are not a problem on their own, but should prompt you to ask yourself, what are his reasons for wanting to take on a new look.

Hang-ups   It has happened to all of us at one time or another. We pick up the phone to hear only silence, or perhaps the sound of the caller hanging up the phone. Sometimes this can be a case of a simple misdialed number. It could also be someone calling for your husband or boyfriend who hangs up once they hear a female voice answer the phone. If it happens once, it's no big deal. If it is happening on a regular basis, it is cause for concern.

Housekeeping   Some men are slobs and others are rather tidy. If you see a change in the way your significant other takes care of his home or apartment, you should take notice. This is especially true for couples that do not live together, as the cheater will be more likely to engage in illicit activity in his own home. If his place is usually a pigsty, but he has suddenly taken more interest in keeping it neat, it may be a sign that he has been having company over.

Hugging   Lets face it, some people are huggers, and others are not. Touching is a part of intimacy, and an element of all relationships. If your partner seems to be hugging you less, you may have a problem. He may be withdrawing from you on a certain level, or he may be paranoid as to what you may sense or smell if he allows you to get too close.

Hygiene   As we have discussed earlier, any changes or improvements in the way that he takes care of his overall appearance and hygiene should raise a question in your mind. This includes all aspects of cleanliness. I don't think I need to go into any further detail here.

Instant Messenger   Communication by way of computer has become commonplace in the electronic age. Using an instant messenger on the Internet can be a more clandestine way of communicating then talking on the phone. It can also have the same appeal for cheaters as it does for teens. Some people will be a little more bold or outgoing when talking to someone by way of Instant Messenger, as opposed to talking on the telephone or face-to-face.

Intimacy   Or more importantly, a lack of intimacy, is an issue. It is a basic requirement that all human beings yearn for. If your husband or boyfriend has become more distant and avoids intimate contact with you, you may wonder if those needs are being fulfilled elsewhere.

Jewelry   Wearing a new piece of jewelry is another sign of vanity. The item does not necessarily need to be new, but perhaps something that he has not been wearing for a while. If he suddenly starts wearing an earring, it may be a misguided attempt to appear younger.

Kissing   As with hugging, kissing is an important part of intimacy. Lack of kissing demonstrates a withdrawal on his part, and should be reason for concern on many levels.   The cheater may also be paranoid and subconsciously fear that you could actually *taste* another woman on his lips.

Laundry   Okay, some men do laundry. It's not that uncommon for men to do their share of the household chores. If, however, he has never done laundry before, I would be suspicious if he suddenly began taking it upon himself to do so. Doing laundry is a simple way to eliminate any stains or smells of infidelity, not only on his clothing, but also on the bedding.

Lipstick   Alright, I admit it, this one is so cliché that I am almost embarrassed to include it.   But lipstick, spotted on a collar, a lip or a cheek can be rather conclusive evidence of unfaithfulness.

Lunch Most people partake of a midday meal at some point during the course of the day. You may find that your partner has not been taking lunch with him to work as often as he used to and may be going out to lunch on a more regular basis. It is rare to do this by yourself. Although his lunch companions may simply be a group of coworkers, he may also be going on a lunch date.

M.O. If you have ever watched any type of police or crime drama on television, you have probably heard the term M.O. It is police lingo and stands for *modus operandi,* which is Latin and loosely translates to method of operation. Detectives will often try to link multiple crimes because they have a similar M.O. If your cheater is a repeat offender, you should look for similarities between his current activity and his past offenses.

Mail Any unusual envelopes or packages that your partner receives should be noted. Try to ascertain the sender by way of a return address, or at least make a note of the postmark to see where the item was sent from.

Makeup This item falls under the same category as lipstick, but may be harder to spot. While lipstick can often be brightly colored pinks and reds, other types of makeup, such as mascara, eyeliner and foundation usually come in more subtle colors such as black, brown or tan and therefore may be more difficult to notice.

Meetings Company functions where his presence is mandatory are a great excuse to explain an absence. In this way, the cheater can always claim that he is not spending time away from you by choice, but because he is required to do so by his employer. Many jobs include meetings, but most are held during regular business hours. Nighttime meetings and out of town meetings, while not unheard of, are certainly less common.

Mileage   Take note of the odometer reading on your partner's car. If he just uses the vehicle to travel back and forth to work, he will generally put about the same amount of mileage on it everyday. You should be able to roughly estimate the distance he travels to his place of work. You can also use a computer service that gives directions, such as www.MapQuest.com, to estimate his round-trip travel mileage. Watch for any changes in these numbers, especially on days that you suspect he has been up to no good.

Mood   You should take note of any changes in your partners overall demeanor. Mood swings or moodiness are indications of some type of underlying problem. You may find that he is in a bad mood when he is at home or spending time with you. This may be a symptom of an unhappy relationship. You may also notice that at times, he is in an overly good mood. This would be extremely suspicious if it occurred immediately preceding or directly following a suspicious absence.

Music   Changes in musical preferences can be an indication that something has changed in his life. When checking out the car, turn the key on and see if the stereo is tuned to a different type of radio station then he usually listens to. Also be aware if the radio is turned off. Most people listen to the radio in the car and leave it on when they turn off the ignition.

Additionally, most people will keep the radio turned down or turned off completely when they have a passenger in the car, or when they are talking on their cell phone. People can have a deep emotional connection with music in general or to a specific song. I'm sure there are songs that remind you of a certain someone from your past. If he seems to be listening to a specific song on a regular basis, it may be that he is thinking of someone else. It's an ironic twist to the old saying. He might not be playing our song, but rather he is playing *their* song.

Office As we discussed previously, the workplace is a prime location for the initiation of a clandestine affair. People interact and work closely together, often for several hours at a time. Any changes in his work schedule, habits, or even attitudes towards his job may be a sign of a love interest at work.

Perfume Have you ever noticed that you are unaware of the smell of the perfume that you are wearing? You smell it when you first put it on, but after the first few minutes, you become oblivious to it. The same is true, if you have another person's perfume on your clothing. He may not be aware of it, but it will definitely be apparent to you the moment he walks through the door.

Personality As with all changes in attitude, you should also be on the lookout for a change in your partner's personality. You may find yourself saying things like "he just doesn't seem like himself" or "this is not the same man I married". For every change in personality, whether subtle or drastic, there is an underlying root cause. Ask yourself what other changes have taken place concurrent with the personality change.

Pet hair If neither you nor your partner owns a pet, you would be justified in being suspicious if you were to find dog or cat hair on his clothing. If you do own a pet, keep in mind that they can often tell if a person has been around another animal by the scent left on the clothing. If you have a dog, I'm sure you have witnessed this firsthand when your dog literally goes wild anytime he picks up the scent of another dog on you.

Phone Telephone usage will usually increase when a person is carrying on an affair. If he seems to be talking on the phone in a secretive manner, or in hushed tones, this is a danger sign. You may also notice that he tends to make phone calls late at night after you have gone to bed, or when you are in the shower or otherwise preoccupied. Additionally, he may quickly end a phone call when you unexpectedly walk into the room.

Phone bill The monthly telephone bill can often hold a considerable amount of incriminating evidence. Be on the lookout for phone calls to unfamiliar numbers, as well as calls of long duration or at strange times. If you are married, or otherwise cohabitate with your partner, you should have easy access to the monthly statement. Be aware of the billing date, and when the statement usually arrives in the mail. If your partner is concerned that you may see unusual call activity on the bill, he may try to get to the mail before you do. In the case of cell phone bills, they offer additional information that landline bills do not. Cell phone usage is billed by minutes used, regardless of whether the call was incoming or outgoing. Therefore, a cell phone bill may list phone numbers of incoming phone calls. A website may also be listed on the bill with information on how to view your monthly call activity online, as well as past month's statements.

Politeness   Would you consider your partner to be a generally polite person, or has he seemed to be more polite of late? If this aspect of his attitude towards you or others has changed, you should take note. It may be another sign of underlying guilt.

Purchases   All expenditures that seem out of the ordinary are worth examining. Tokens of affection and other gifts usually must be purchased either by cash, check or credit card. Also be aware of purchases that seem out of character, or are aimed at changing his image, i.e., new clothing, jewelry, sports car, etc.

Questions   Every cheater dreads having to answer certain questions. An unfaithful partner will avoid conversations and topics that would prompt you to ask those questions. He may also avoid asking questions of you, or seem otherwise disinterested for the same reasons. If he asks "How was your day?" or inquires about your whereabouts, he could expect to be asked the same type of questions by you. Questions he may not want to answer.

Receipts   A key element of any paper trail is a printed receipt. Every purchase, restaurant check, or bar tab involves a receipt documenting the transaction. If you come across any unusual receipts, take note of all of the data contained on it. The date, time, and location can be incriminating information by itself. Even a seemingly innocent purchase, such as buying gasoline, could be incriminating if the transaction took place at a time and location that does not correspond with your partner's explanation of his whereabouts.

Restaurants   The act of courtship often involves sharing a meal. Look for signs that your partner has been frequenting restaurants. Besides a receipt, you may notice books of matches with the restaurant's name and location printed on them. Although not a clue to its specific location, if you should notice items such as cellophane wrapped toothpicks or red and white striped mints mixed in with his pocket change, this is a sign that he has recently visited a restaurant.

Routine   We all have daily rituals and regular routines that we adhere to without even thinking about it. This can apply to just about any aspect of life. If you notice that your husband or boyfriend has recently changed his routine in any way, this may be a cause for concern.

Rudeness   If a man is unhappy with the relationship that he is currently in, he will often find ways to push his partner away and begin to distance himself from the relationship.   This usually takes place on an unconscious level, but can manifest itself in many types of behavior, including rudeness.

Schedule   People have all types of schedules. Work schedules, exercise schedules, dog walking schedules, and the list goes on and on. Look for any deviation in your partner's regular schedules or routines. If he suddenly is required to work nights or on weekends, this could be a cover for some other type of activity. An affair involves two people, not just one, so keep in mind that two schedules must be aligned in order for those two people to be able to spend time together. The other woman may be married or otherwise attached also, making her schedule a challenge as well. The bottom line is that your partner may have to change his routine to accommodate the other person's schedule.

Secrecy If your mate seems overly secretive about any aspect of his life, you should begin to wonder what it is he is hiding. The secrecy can be about anything really, so you shouldn't just focus your attention on activities that seem inherently suspicious. In a healthy relationship, there should be little or no secrets.

Security If your partner is becoming concerned that the other woman is becoming obsessed with him or overly jealous of his home life, he may begin to show more interest in home security. Most people have seen the movie *Fatal Attraction*, and I think just about every unfaithful man out there must have that rattling around somewhere in the back of their mind.

Sex Any changes in your partners sexual habits, attitudes, or behavior is worth noting. Your sex life will usually change when your partner is involved in an extracurricular relationship. The change can be severe, or very subtle, and range from one extreme to the other. He may become disinterested in engaging in sexual activity with you if he is sexually active elsewhere, or his level of interest in sex may become elevated, as he becomes preoccupied with thoughts of another woman.

Shaving Most men have a set time and place when they tend to shaving their faces. As with all grooming habits, you should be aware if he becomes more concerned with his appearance. You can usually spot a freshly shaved face and can definitely feel it with a simple touch of the hand. If he begins to shave before going out in the evening, that may be a bad sign.

Showering Once again, any change in his routine regarding his overall level of cleanliness should be noted. As with shaving, if he showers before going out in the evening he is taking extra measures to be clean. On the flip side, if he takes a shower upon returning home from a suspicious absence, he may be trying to eliminate evidence on his person. You should also be aware if he returns home with a slightly wet hair, or other signs of a recent shower, in the event that he took a shower at another location.

Sleep habits   Some people are sound sleepers and others suffer from insomnia. Watch and listen for any change in your partners sleeping patterns. Difficulty in falling asleep, as well as restlessness while sleeping can be indicative that something is on his mind. Anxiety and guilt can often be common causes of insomnia.

Smells   They say that the sense of smell is the strongest of the five human senses. Take notice of any unusual odors on him when he returns home from work or any other absence. You may notice the smell of perfume, baby powder, baby oil or moisturizing lotion on his body. When two people engage in skin to skin contact, the scent of one will undoubtedly rub off on the other. Therefore, any toiletry products used by the other woman have the potential to be transferred onto your partner. You should also keep a nose out for odors on his laundry or coat, and inside his car. Body odor, or a musky smell, can be the result of recent physical exertion.

Smoking   Changes in your partner's tobacco usage can be good reason to take notice. If he is a former smoker, he may begin to smoke again if he is in the company of another smoker. If he is not a smoker, you should be highly suspicious if his clothing or car smells of cigarette smoke. Obviously, this would indicate that he has been in close proximity of someone who smokes.

On the other hand, if he does smoke, and he is involved with another woman who is a non-smoker, he may curtail his smoking if she finds it to be offensive. I once knew a man who was a smoker for several years. During that time he dated a woman who did not smoke and was repulsed by the smell of it. He would never smoke around her, and would always shower, brush his teeth, and put on clean clothing before going on a date with her.

Socializing   Having an affair is a social activity and will often go hand-in-hand with other social behavior. If he is going out with his friends more often than he used to, or frequenting bars or other social locations, take note. This is especially true if you are not invited to accompany him or feel otherwise unwelcome at these social gatherings. It may also be a sign that he is looking for opportunities to cheat.

Solitude   You should be very concerned if you notice that your husband or partner is beginning to spend an increasing amount of time by himself. This is a sign that he is withdrawing from you and you are justified in being worried. He may also be using this solitary time to communicate with someone else by way of the telephone or computer. If he is going out by himself with the explanation that he wants to spend some time alone, there is a good chance that he is doing anything but.

Spam   Have you ever noticed the ridiculous amount of junk e-mail that you receive on a daily basis? Companies that market by way of the Internet will purchase lists of e-mail addresses of people who have visited certain types of websites. In that way, they can market their product or service to people who fit a certain demographic or group. If you are noticing an increased amount of spam in your shared e-mail box advertising dating websites, how to meet women or any sexually explicit topics, it is a good sign that someone has been viewing this type of material on that computer.

Stalkers As I mentioned earlier, another woman may be as jealous of you as you are of her. There is always the chance that she could become obsessed with your partner when she realizes that he may not be willing to end his relationship with you in order to be with her. This scenario is not uncommon, as most cheaters will often tell the other woman that a breakup, separation or divorce is imminent. She may become enraged as time goes on, and these promises go un-kept. Although not unheard of, it is somewhat unusual for a woman to stalk a man when he has done nothing to contribute to her actions.

Statements Bank statements, credit card statements, and telephone bills are all valuable ways to gather information about a person's movements, habits and activities. Closely scrutinize any such statements that you are able to view.

Style Any changes to your partners overall style may be completely innocent or may be cause for concern. As mentioned earlier, a change of hairstyle or wardrobe can be a sign that he is trying to change his image or otherwise present himself in a more appealing or attractive manner. More so than any other time in their relationship, a man will try to please a woman most during the initial courting process. He will be much more open to suggestions and willing to make changes to please his partner. He may be willing to try new things at the suggestion of another woman, even though he would not be receptive to the same suggestion if it were to come from you.

Text messaging   Personally, I find it rather tedious to use my cell phone's touch pad to send text messages to others. I would rather just make the phone call and speak to someone, but that's just me. I know that I am in the minority. One advantage of text messaging that a cheater will exploit is that he can easily carry on a conversation with another woman without the risk that someone may be eavesdropping on him. A cell phone is also a much more portable device than say, a computer, making it easy to text message someone from the bathroom or some other secluded location.

Trash   Any experienced private investigator will tell you that you can learn more about a person and their activities by looking through their garbage than by any other probative technique. Yes, I know that this can be a dirty and smelly undertaking, but you will be amazed at what you can learn as a result of your efforts. Just think about it, there is evidence of just about everything we do in our trash. And even more importantly, what will a cheater do with evidence that he does not want you to see? The answer is quite simple; he will throw it out.   If he is extra cautious, he will take the incriminating items elsewhere for disposal, or use a paper shredder if available, but most average people will simply throw it away. One minor precaution that some men will take is to take the item in question outside of the home to the trashcan, rather than leave it in a wastebasket inside the house. This precaution can be easily defeated by not only searching the garbage inside the house, but also the outside trashcans. A good time to do this is right before garbage pickup, as a skilled cheater will often wait until the last minute to dispose of evidence.

Travel   Where has your partner been and where is he planning to go? If he has never traveled for his job in the past, but suddenly has to go out of town on business, you may be justified in questioning his intentions.   A cheater can use any one of countless excuses for going away overnight or for a couple of days.   He may not be going away at all, but simply shacking up at the other woman's residence. If he *is* going out of town, it could possibly be for a romantic getaway.   One interesting scenario has become more and more prevalent over the past several years.   As people meet, and even carry on, virtual relationships on the Internet, there will often be considerable distance between the two parties' actual physical locations.   In the beginning of this type of experimental relationship, the lack of proximity may seem like a form of safety net, as both people know that they are not that likely to meet in person.   As the cyber relationship becomes more serious, whether real or imagined, the desire for a face-to-face interlude may become much stronger.

Underwear   Most likely, you are fairly familiar with the type of underwear that your partner usually wears. If you notice that he has changed the type of underwear that he is wearing, you should take note. He may not change the style, but perhaps purchase some new ones if the old ones were getting raggedy or dingy.   You should also be aware if he has recently changed to a sexier type of underwear. Many men will have some older underwear and some nicer underwear mixed in their drawer. You should monitor the laundry to see if his underwear wearing habits correspond to any other patterns noted in your journal.

Vagueness If your husband or partner seems more evasive when you discuss his activities or whereabouts, you have reason to be suspicious. Liars and cheats will often be vague in their answers as they are buying time to try to come up with an acceptable excuse.

Vanity Although it is a term that is most often associated with the female of our species, men can be just as vain as women. They may try to conceal their vanity more so than women, but it is still evident. If your husband or boyfriend seems to be more interested in his physical appearance, he may be trying to impress someone.

Wedding ring If you are married to your partner, the rings that you wear are a symbol of your love and commitment to one another. If you notice that your husband is not wearing his wedding ring, you should be wondering why. It is one thing if he should, for some reason forget to put it on, or does not wear it during certain activities such as yard work, or playing sports. If he goes to work with his wedding ring on, but comes home with it in his pocket, that is a definite danger sign.

Getting the Goods On Him

Before we can catch him and find absolute proof of his infidelity, we must begin to narrow the search a little bit. Although you should try to have a heightened level of awareness at all times, you can't be looking in every direction or at every situation for evidence. This can be extremely counterproductive. Not only will it take a long time, but it will probably make you frantic in the process. You may already be acutely aware of this very fact. Obviously, you did not get to this point overnight. You have probably spent days, weeks, or even months, suspecting that something is amiss in your relationship.

You must begin to focus your investigative efforts towards specific times and circumstances that you feel that there is an increased likelihood that illicit activity is taking place. With that in mind, we will focus on three key questions; when, where, and how. As I have mentioned earlier, why is a question that may help determine if an affair is taking place, but for the purposes of catching a cheater, that question is irrelevant. Quite frankly, why someone cheats should be the topic of a whole other book, one that I am not qualified to write.

The first and probably the most important question you must ask yourself is when. When is the infidelity taking place? We must be able to focus our attention on a specific timeframe or at least a list of specific time frames in which you believe that your partner is being unfaithful. You should take into consideration that a week consists of 168 hours. Of that time, the activity in question is probably only taking place during one to five hours per week. The time involved may be considerably greater if communication by way of computer is a component of the relationship.

The time that we are focusing on should not be limited to those hours in which your partner could possibly be meeting the other woman in person. We must also focus on time spent communicating with one another, such as phone conversations, text messaging and time spent on the computer. To the other extreme, some affairs may only involve one or two face-to-face encounters per month, with little or no communication or interaction between meetings.

As always, you should take note of any patterns forming as to times of suspicious or unexplained absences. Surprisingly, many cheaters will have set patterns as to when they meet with the other woman. They will also often have a preset schedule of when to "meet" on the Internet. In other cases, the time of in person meetings will be totally random and only scheduled at a time when both parties feel that they can safely get away.

You should remember that the other woman has a schedule as well. A rendezvous may be scheduled based on her availability more so than his. She may have a work schedule to consider as well as other obligations. Perhaps she is being unfaithful to her own husband or boyfriend, making the coordination of their two schedules even more difficult.

Many cheaters are opportunistic and will seize a spontaneous opportunity when it arises. Others will take advantage of what used to be a legitimate absence and use it for other purposes. If you unexpectedly have to work late, or go visit a sick relative, this may give him the chance to sneak away for an illicit encounter. Of course, "staging" a fictitious opportunity can produce great results from an investigative standpoint. By giving him an unexpected opportunity, you will know exactly when to focus your efforts. We will discuss that method in a later chapter.

Once you know when to look, you can try to determine where the activity is taking place. The locale in which a person will carry on an affair will usually be close, but not too close. Close enough to be convenient, yet far enough away to avoid detection. Most cheaters will try to conduct in person meetings with the other woman in places that are outside their own, or their partners, sphere of influence.

If they are meeting socially for drinks, or to share lunch or dinner, the location of the meeting may vary greatly. If they are meeting for a sexual encounter, the location of those meetings will usually be the same. He may be meeting her at her house or apartment, especially if she is single and lives alone. If she is married or otherwise attached, they would be more likely to meet at a hotel. A cheater knows that he is doing something wrong, so he will use the same location over and over again if he has gone undetected in the past. Many affairs will fall into a pattern and be so regular that you can set your watch by them. They will often take place at the same time and place, week after week. You should also consider your husband or boyfriend's personality. If he is extremely predictable in his daily routines, that character trait will carry over into his extracurricular activities.

It is not unheard of for a habitual or serial cheater to keep a separate apartment for the purpose of clandestine meetings with other women. The location and very existence of this apartment may be a very closely guarded secret. I have worked cases where I discovered that a group of men, all married by the way, shared the rent and expenses of keeping up an apartment for the sole purpose of cheating on their wives. It was quite an elaborate set up they had going there, and even had a schedule in place as to who would use the apartment on what days.

Some businessmen will keep a separate apartment that is closer to their office if he lives a considerable distance away. In this way, he can sleep at the apartment on days where he needs to work late, in order to cut down on excessive commuting time. An example of this would be the married man who lives in the suburbs of a major city, but has an apartment *in town* that is near work. I have also seen instances where a man will maintain the apartment that he lived in before the couple married and moved into a shared space, for the same reasons. Even if your husband or boyfriend is keeping an apartment for what he claims to be, or once was, a legitimate purpose, it does afford him a tremendous opportunity to stray. At least you will have a good idea as to where and when to focus your attention. Of these cases, many can be exactly what they are portrayed to be, with no malfeasance involved. Keep in mind that maintaining such an apartment is a considerable expense that most people would not be willing to take on. You should know if your partner is in a financial position to afford such an expense.

The final question that we need to answer is how. How the infidelity is taking place can be a more difficult question to answer. For our purposes, *how* can be a very broad term indeed. In the first place, *how* can refer to the type of infidelity and what type of behavior you consider acceptable or unacceptable. He may be physically meeting with someone and possibly engaging in sexual activity. He may also be meeting with someone socially, for example; meeting for drinks or dinner. Perhaps the affair is taking place right under your nose, online, in the form of a virtual or *cyber-relationship*. So answering the question of how also includes an explanation of what is taking place.

In the second place, *how* can refer to; how is he creating the opportunity for the affair. He may be making excuses to allow his absences or inventing fictitious circumstances or activities to explain them. In some cases, he may be carrying on an affair with a coworker and the infidelity is solely occurring at his workplace. In this case, it can be more difficult to detect the affair because his absence from you is perfectly normal and understandable. Many affairs will begin in the office, but escalate to spending time together during nonworking hours.

Cheaters are creatures of habit and will use and repeat the same methods and explanations over and over again if they have worked in the past. He will stick to his tried and true methods as long as he believes that you do not suspect him. For this reason, you should try to conceal your suspicions so that he will continue following the same patterns. If he knows you are on to him, he will change his methods and it will be harder to catch him in the act. Additionally, he may continue to use the same explanations, simply because it is easier to remember one lie than many lies. He will basically stick to the same story.

As far as getting the goods on him, understanding his past behavior will give you a great deal of insight and will help you to predict when, where, and how he will do it again. Even if he is not a typical cheater, and there is no pattern and his actions are totally random, you will be able to recognize the indicators and know enough to suspect that he is up to no good. In any case, the next time it happens you will be prepared to get the goods on him.

Once again, I cannot stress enough the importance of using a journal or some other method to document his activities and all suspicious behavior. Over time, the answers to when, where, and how will all become apparent in the pages of your journal. As you begin to discover clues and gather evidence, it is extremely important that you do your best to remain calm and collected until you have collected enough information to be certain as to what has been going on. The moment your partner knows that you suspect, your task will become ten times more difficult. You should also know that one clue usually leads to another, and another. Take your time and follow the evidence to wherever it leads you.

The Rules of Evidence

By this point, you should have a good idea of what to look for and whether or not you have reasonable grounds to be suspicious. You should also have a good idea as to what areas you need to focus your attention on in an attempt to gather tangible evidence of infidelity. What we are looking for now, simply put, is proof. You want to know for yourself, with an absolute certainty, that your partner is being unfaithful. If you plan to confront him, you cannot leave any room for him to explain away what you have uncovered. It must be conclusive. For this reason, you must always wait until you have that absolute degree of certainty before moving forward with any type of action against your partner. Once you reveal that you have done a fine job of investigative work and know what he has been up to, you can be sure that he will not make the same mistakes again and it will be 10 times harder to get any evidence against him in the future.

That brings us to an interesting question. We know that we are looking for absolute proof of his actions, but to whom do we need to prove it? This is the appropriate time for you to ask this question of yourself. If your reasons for seeking proof are only for your own peace of mind so that you can make future decisions about your relationship with confidence, then the burden of proof is considerably less. For example, if you were to catch your partner coming out of a hotel room with another woman, I don't think that would leave any questions in your mind as to what was going on inside. If however, you are married and your subsequent probing may lead to a divorce proceeding, you may need more tangible proof and documentation of your partner's infidelity. In divorce court, any attorney worth his or her fee can quickly portray your observations as blind and jealous accusations and claim that there is no basis in truth. In layman's terms, the divorce proceeding will be reduced to a simple case of "he said, she said". I have seen many divorce cases over the years, and believe me, you do not want to find yourself in that type of situation.

For most women in your situation, a combination of first-hand knowledge, as well as some form of printed or recorded documentation should be sufficient to not only know that your suspicions have been warranted, but also to stand up in court, if need be. Even if you don't anticipate needing the leverage while negotiating a future property settlement agreement, it is still a good idea to have incontrovertible proof before confronting the cheater. He may try to explain his way out of a single instance of questionable behavior, but let's see him try to tap dance around three or four different pieces of evidence. In the following pages, we will explore a variety of techniques for obtaining the proof that you will need.

Case Study

Janet & Bob

To many of the people who knew them, Janet and Bob's marriage did not necessarily seem like a bad one. It just didn't seem like a particularly happy one, either. The couple had been married for 22 years and raised three children together, a boy and two girls. Meredith, the oldest of the three, was in her freshman year at Rutgers, but still lived at home. Robbie and Kate both attended River Edge high school in the quiet northern New Jersey town.

Bob made the commute into Manhattan each day, to his job at a major New York City accounting firm. He'd been with the company for 12 years now, and his position was secure. He never quite lived up to the expectations that the firm had for him when he was first hired, but all things considered, he did an adequate job. He earned a good salary and received annual increases that afforded the family a comfortable, upper-middle-class lifestyle.

Janet was a homemaker and had stopped working when Meredith was born. She felt fortunate to be able to be a stay-at-home mom, and be actively involved in her children's lives. She was a class mother when the kids were in elementary school, and was now kept quite busy shuttling Robbie and Kate back and forth to their numerous practices and social activities. Both children were always involved in something, to Janet's delight, as she was never much of a *joiner* herself when she was that age. Meredith had taken after her in that regard, and did not get involved in sports or school events. All three were good kids, and she was so proud to see them developing into fine, young adults.

Many of Janet and Bob's friends silently speculated that the couple had remained together all of these years for the children. After all, they just never seemed to have much in common. When they would all go out for dinner, there never seemed to be much interaction between the two. Bob would talk with the men about business and sports, and Janet and the ladies would always talk about their kids. Even when they were together, they're always appeared to be a distance between them. They just never seemed to be as close as the other couples were.

Although she didn't think about it much at the time, Janet would later realize in retrospect, that the couple simply stayed together out of complacency. They weren't really unhappy, and financially, they didn't want for anything. It's just the way that things had always been and the idea of splitting up had never even entered Janet's mind. She was content with her life and Bob seemed content with his. He spent long hours at the office and would often grab something to eat in the city. He never worked on weekends though, and was always there for his children when they needed him.

With the kids growing older, they were starting to spend more time out of the house and exploring life on their own. This was a good thing, Janet thought, and the normal course of nature. She had watched as Meredith had spread her wings and begun to go out on her own and Robbie would be next. He already had his permit and would be taking his license test in less than two months. Janet was beginning to fear the empty nest that was looming in the not too distant future, but she knew there was nothing she could do about it. She was already feeling as if she had too much time on her hands as it was.

She had always been a meticulous housekeeper and enjoyed tending to her flower gardens. She decided to do some sprucing up around the house with her newfound free time. She began by cleaning out the basement and reorganizing the attic. One look into the detached garage was all it took for Janet to decide to leave well enough alone. There had to be all sorts of spiders and things living in there amongst the clutter. And besides, they had not used it to park her car in for years. There were plenty of other projects that she could tackle around the house and she would leave the garage to the spiders for now.

When Janet turned her attention to cleaning out all of the closets in the home, she could not believe how much old clothing she found. There were plenty of clothes that she knew the kids would never wear again, and countless suits and sportcoats that Bob was unlikely to ever fit in again. By the time she finished the closets, she had filled 12 hefty bags with used clothing that she would bring to the Salvation Army in the morning. She was enjoying cleaning out the house and felt productive. Until she started digging into it, she hadn't realized just how overdue some of these chores had become.

Probably the messiest room in the house was Bob's den. It was a good size room off the front parlor with pocket doors that could be closed for privacy. This came in handy to hide the cluttered room on the rare occasions that the couple would have guests. Bob didn't use the room often except during tax season when he would spend countless hours at the large mahogany desk that sat in front of the bay window.

For the most part, the room was Bob's catch all. There were mountains of papers and trade journals and haphazardly stacked piles of who knows what. She always wondered how he could ever find anything in there. She would try to dust and vacuum in the den as best she could, moving the mounds of clutter from place to place as she cleaned.

It was a gloomy Tuesday morning, when Janet decided to tackle the den. She had planned on going to the mall to do a little shopping, but when she awoke to rain, she decided to stay in for the day. It was a decision that would change her life forever. She figured that she could sort through the clutter on the desk first, and at least try to get it somewhat organized. Although there was a file cabinet in the room, most of the records seemed to end up on a pile somewhere rather than being filed away. She used to help Bob with filing and other miscellaneous paperwork when they were first married, so she had no reservations about organizing the desk.

By noontime, she had over 30 different stacks of paper all over the desk, the sofa, and the floor. It may have looked worse than when she started, but Janet knew better. Most of the papers had been sorted by category and would only need to be filed in the appropriate folder in the filing cabinet. There were all sorts of bills and statements and invoices. Some was business related, but most of the paperwork was their personal records. Mortgage statements, utility bills, canceled checks, credit cards, etc. It was all there.

Now that everything had been sorted, she began to focus her attention on filing it away. It seemed like the next logical step, until she opened the first of the three filing cabinet drawers to discover that it was already full. She knew she should've checked the drawers first, but shrugged it off and began to thumb through the contents of the files. Some of the folders contained records dating back over 10 years. She knew that this was the main cause for the abundance of papers in the den, since nothing had been thrown out for such a long period of time. She would have to dig through and throw out the old records so she would have room to file the more recent ones.

One of the drawers contained two shoeboxes filled with nothing but canceled checks. She knew that you should always keep financial records for at least seven years in case you are audited, but some of these checks dated back considerably further. She would have to sort through the checks and shred the older ones. As she thumbed through each stack of checks, it became increasingly difficult to ignore the payee's name on the front. Most of them were far from interesting, a water bill or mortgage payment. Yet others told a story. A communion gift for Jim and Betty's oldest son. A check payable to the hospital from when Meredith had her tonsils removed. It was a strange walk down memory lane as Janet continued to sort through the checks. As she continued, she began to notice something rather unusual. She consistently found checks made out to *The Windsor Apartments, LLC*. She thought it was strange when she came across the first one, but became more and more puzzled as she found that there was a check paid to them every month.

As she proceeded, she discovered that a payment had been made to The Windsor Apartments, dated the first of every month for the past six years. The checks started at $600 per month and had increased gradually over time to $835 per month. Janet was flabbergasted and was not sure what to make of her discovery. As she dug deeper through the piles of checks, she began to notice more than one electric bill per month. After about two hours of digging, there was only one conclusion that made sense. Bob was paying the rent, electric, and water bill on an apartment at The Windsor Apartments.

A quick call to information revealed that The Windsor Apartments were located in Dumont, a small town only about 5 miles away. During the next several hours, Janet carefully examined every piece of paper in the den and was able to document a trail of deceit that dated back almost a decade...

Following the Paper Trail

We live in a world that keeps a record of many of the things that we do during the course of our everyday lives. Any transaction that involves money will certainly leave documentation behind. Every purchase, whether by cash, check, ATM card or credit card will leave a paper trail. For our purposes, we will also consider *paperless documentation* as a part of the paper trail, since many companies, banks and financial institutions have begun to eliminate actual paper documents. I guess for now, we will have to keep using the term until someone comes up with something better.

One of the key elements of any affair is money. It is rare to see any romantic relationship that does not cost money in one way or another. Drinks are bought, hotel rooms are paid for, and gifts are exchanged all in the course of carrying on an affair. For this reason, the paper trail is one of the most common ways that a cheater's infidelity is ultimately discovered.

The first thing that you should be keeping an eye out for in your investigative efforts is a simple receipt. Printed paper receipts, regardless of the purchase, are often viewed to be a nuisance and are treated as trash. How many times have you made a purchase and shoved the receipt into your pocket, wallet, or purse, along with the change and completely forgotten about it? Unless you believe that there is a chance that you will be returning the item in question, the receipt will probably be thrown out or otherwise discarded.

While a woman will usually put a receipt in her purse, a man will usually put a receipt in his wallet or loose in his pocket. This is where knowing your partner's habits will come in handy to help you track down this type of evidence. Some men will empty the contents of their pockets onto the dresser before undressing. Others have a habit of leaving miscellaneous items in their pockets. Do you find crumpled up and illegible pieces of paper in the washing machine after laundering your husband's or boyfriends clothing? Does he keep his car neat, or is it filled with candy bar wrappers and scraps of paper? In general, the sloppier the man, the easier it is to find incriminating evidence in this way.

Check his dresser, pockets, the place where he keeps his car keys, and the car it self for any clues. You can also have a look in his wallet if the opportunity presents itself, or in his briefcase, if he carries one. There may be a drawer in his desk or night table that acts as a catchall for whatever comes home in his pockets each day. Again, where you look will greatly depend on your partner's personality and his daily habits.

Beyond the receipt itself, you should also begin to analyze any monthly statements that you have access to. This will include bank statements, credit card bills, and anything else that you feel may be relevant. You should be aware of what method of payment your partner commonly uses to make purchases. Does he use an ATM card to buy gas, or perhaps he always uses his credit card when paying at a restaurant, to make it easier to add the gratuity. Maybe your guy is the old-fashioned cash only type. Once again, take into account his typical way of doing things.

Bank statements and credit card bills usually come by mail. If you are married or cohabitate with your partner, you'll probably have easier access to these types of items. You may have to try to beat him to the mailbox to get the first look at any statements that may arrive. If you do not live with your partner, you will have to keep an eye out for open statements around the house. Most men will have one place where they keep and pay their bills.

While we are looking for statements, it is important to know what statements we should actually be looking for. Check his wallet to see what credit cards he carries, and also have a look at his checkbook register to see what credit card companies he is making payments to. You may only be aware of the MasterCard that you both carry from your joint account, but he may have an additional card that you are unaware of. I have seen some habitual cheater's who have a second credit card that they keep secret from their wives or girlfriends by having the bill sent to their office or another alternative location.

Another way to conceal bank or credit card records is to only receive the monthly statement online, by way of e-mail. Even if he does receive a monthly bill or statement by way of the US mail, you should also keep in mind that this information is often readily available online. If you do have access to a paper statement, check to see if it lists a website for that particular bank or financial institution.

Regardless of what documents you are able to find, take note of everything. What may seem irrelevant now, may turn out to be a critical piece of information once you start to piece together the puzzle.

Many cheaters will make purchases online to avoid detection, only to overlook the item when their credit card statement arrives. Don't just look at what was purchased and the business that it was purchased from, but also take note of the time, date, and location of the purchase. You can cross check this information against your journal to see if it corresponds with any unexplained absences. The date and time of a seemingly innocent transaction could contradict where he had previously claimed to be.

In the end, the final resting place of any paper trail is always the trash. Garbage can be an abundant source of information. Detectives will commonly refer to this technique as *dumpster diving*. If you don't believe me as to the value of a person's trash, try having a look at your own. You may be surprised at what you find.

The first step will of course be to get a hold of your partner's garbage. As always, if you are married, this won't be as hard to do. If you don't live with him, I'm sure you can devise a plan to "steal" his garbage. The trash from a wastepaper basket located near a desk will often yield better results than a kitchen garbage can full of coffee grounds and carrot tops. If he uses a paper shredder, the chances of finding anything worthwhile will be substantially less. If all of the garbage from your partner's house is mixed together, you'll just have to dig in and deal with it. Spread out some hefty bags on the floor and get started. You may want to use a pair of dishwashing gloves if you like. I assure you that you will be amazed at the amount of information that you can uncover in this way. All of the documents that we have mentioned in this chapter could potentially end up in the trash and bear the evidence that you are seeking.

8

The Car

One place that many people often overlook in their search for tangible evidence is the subject's vehicle. People spend a great deal of time in their car and will often leave clues behind that they would not overlook in their home. You should keep in mind that the car may be an integral part of your partner's relationship with the other woman. At the very least, there is a good chance that he is traveling to meet her, and doing so by car. At most, the other woman herself may have spent time in his car and left behind a variety of clues.

It may be difficult to find an opportunity to inspect your husband or boyfriend's vehicle without his knowledge. This is simply because when he goes out, he would most likely take his car. You will have to look for another chance to get a look inside. He may go out for a run, or go somewhere with a friend. Your only opportunity may be while he is asleep or in the shower.

Once in the car, the first thing you should do is take a deep breath in through your nose to try to detect any odor or fragrance that may be in the car. It is best to do this when you first get in, as you will have the best chance to smell anything unusual in the first 15 seconds or so. I know this will sound strange, but the next thing you should do is put your face down close to the passenger seat. As you know, a woman may wear a variety of products on her body at any given time, including perfume, moisturizers, body spray and hand creams. These products may be transferred to the car's upholstery from her clothing or her bare legs if she is wearing a skirt.

While you are focusing your attention on the passenger seat of the vehicle, you should also note the position of the seat and how it is adjusted. Sit on the passenger side of the car to see if the seat seems any different from the way it usually is when you are the passenger. You may want to adjust the seat a little differently before moving on. Set the seat back to a slightly more upright position to make it just a little bit uncomfortable. Your partner will not notice the difference, and even if he did, he would not be able to reach the controls while he is driving. You will be able to check back at a later time to see if the seat has been adjusted. This will be a good indication if someone has been a passenger in the car recently.

Next, you should move to the driver's side of the vehicle and sit behind the wheel. Turn the ignition on and check the car's odometer. Note the mileage and make an entry in your journal. You should have a good idea of how far your partner should be driving during the course of a typical day. Excessive mileage could be an indication that he is going places that you are unaware of. By beginning to keep a regular record of the vehicle's odometer readings, you will be able to cross check it with your journal entries to ensure that the mileage corresponds with your partner's alleged whereabouts. While the ignition is turned on, take note if the radio is on, and if so, what station is it programmed to. Press the eject button to see what CD or cassette is in the stereo. As always, you are looking for anything out of character.

Now turn your attention to any place in the vehicle that you might find a forgotten piece of evidence. Check the coin holder, the cup holder, the console, the pouch on both the driver's door and the passenger door, and the glove compartment. Look for anything that might be of interest such as receipts, written directions, claim checks, toll receipts, or valet parking stubs. You should also look above the sun visor, as many people will stick loose papers up there.

If your partner is not a smoker, look for signs that someone has been smoking in the car. Check the ashtray to see if it has been used and also look for any books of matches that may have been left behind. Even if your partner is a smoker and uses the car's ashtray, check the cigarette butts to see if there are any of a different brand. Countless cases have been broken wide open by a lipstick stained cigarette butt found in an ashtray.

One very simple and low-tech method that has been used for years by traffic enforcement officers and meter maids is *tire marking*. By marking one of the vehicle's tires with a piece of chalk, you will be able to determine if the car has been moved since you last observed it. This will allow you to know if he has been out with just a quick glance and without having to check the odometer for mileage. You should make the mark on the passenger side rear tire so it will be less likely that he will notice it.

9

Telephone Communication

One of the most damning, as well as incontrovertible types of proof that you can get on a cheater is to be able to hear him talking to the other woman or speaking to someone else about her. One of the easiest ways to tap into a line of communication between two parties is to eavesdrop on a telephone conversation.

Although there is a disclaimer included at the beginning of this book, I will take this moment to stress to you that you must familiarize yourself with state and local as well as federal laws regarding listening in or recording another person's phone conversations. Some jurisdictions have substantial penalties for such activities. There may be certain loopholes that you may be able to exploit to avoid violating any laws or incurring any penalties. For example, if you are married or otherwise cohabitate with your partner, you technically could be listening in, or recording conversations on your own phone, as opposed to a telephone belonging to and registered to someone else. Another way that you may be able to stay on the right side of the law is by only listening in or eavesdropping on a telephone conversation, as opposed to electronically recording it. So know and understand the guidelines in your area and proceed with caution. You should use the methods explained in this book only after fully understanding the laws in your area and ensuring that you are in compliance with them. Enough said.

In the following chapters we will focus on hardwired, landline telephones, as they are the easiest, and often times most accessible target for our efforts. With the advent of cellular telephones, many people are using their home phones less and less. Some people, to Ma Bell's dismay, have discontinued their landline telephone service altogether. Still, many continue to use both types of telephones and have active phone service within their home. In this chapter we will start with the basics, such as simple ways that you can use telephone company services as well as the standard features of the telephone itself to gather information. Finally, we will move on to more advanced telephone surveillance techniques and discuss some of the inexpensive equipment that is readily available to you.

Getting the Most
Out of Caller ID

By now, most people are familiar with the caller ID service offered by our local telephone companies. This service has become extremely popular and many landline telephone service customers have opted to add this feature to their service. Caller ID displays data regarding incoming phone calls on a display screen. The screen is either located on the telephone itself or on a separate caller ID unit. The data will include the phone number, as well as date and time of the incoming call. The name that the incoming phone number is registered to will often times be displayed as well.

Whether you cohabitate with your partner or just visit his home, you can familiarize yourself with the caller ID equipped telephone or separate caller ID unit that is in use. If you have access to the owner's manual for the phone, or CID unit, it may be helpful to read through and understand the different features provided. If you are unable to physically look at a hard copy of the owner's manual, you may be able to read the features and directions online by visiting the manufacturer's website.

Keep in mind, that caller ID can easily be defeated by the incoming caller, usually by dialing *67 from the callers telephone. This option may not be available if the caller in question is calling from a cellular phone. Many people mistakenly think that using the *67 feature from their cell phone will block the caller ID data.

When reviewing caller ID data, you should keep an eye out for unfamiliar phone numbers, as well as calls that have been blocked by the caller. These calls will usually appear as *blocked call* or *private call* on the CID display. Remember that this notation means that the caller has intentionally blocked his or her CID information, and the call should be considered somewhat suspicious. You should not be too concerned with calls that say *unknown name* or *out of area*, as these calls will usually be from telemarketers or be generated from large companies.

Do not be fooled into thinking that a call is not suspicious, because it only appears one time in the caller ID history. Many CID units will only show a caller once in the history. It may only show data for the call with the most recent date and time. Any suspicious phone numbers that appear on caller ID can be easily checked by using an online service such as www.whitepages.com. Whitepages.com offers a reverse look-up feature that allows you to enter a phone number and it will tell you to whom it is registered.

Just a note here, you should not only focus your attention on caller ID entries that are unfamiliar to you. You should also be aware of familiar names and numbers that seem to fit into any unusual patterns. It is not uncommon for the other woman to turn out to be someone that you know or are even friends with.

The information obtained from caller ID may not seem that valuable as many cheaters will be well aware that there is a record of his incoming calls, and will therefore take precautions and make a point of deleting the suspicious entries. Although this is a very simple precaution to take, I have found that many people will overlook it at least some of the time.

Let's assume that your partner is extremely diligent in covering his CID tracks, and always makes a point of deleting the entry after receiving a phone call from the other woman. There may be one thing that he has overlooked or simply has not realized. When you delete an entry from a caller ID unit or CID equipped telephone, you are only deleting the entry from that particular unit or phone. Therefore, the incriminating data will still be visible on the other phone extensions or units in the house. Believe it or not, this simple oversight has been the downfall of many cheaters. Many people will have more than one phone extension in their home, and often have phones that they rarely or never use. So when looking for evidence by way of caller ID, don't just check the most accessible and commonly used phone, be sure to check them all.

Installing a Covert
Caller ID Unit

After reading the previous chapter, you may be starting to see a hidden opportunity to gather information. Let's say that your partner is overly cautious, and is always careful to delete the caller ID data from all of the telephones or units in the house. But what if there was a CID unit that he was unaware of? This ridiculously simple tactic has worked on numerous occasions to covertly see who has been calling. If he lives in a studio apartment, this approach would obviously be more challenging. Possible, but challenging.

If he lives in an apartment with multiple rooms or preferably a house, there may be opportunities available to you. Many people have phone jacks in their homes that are unused. Whether it is in your shared home or in his home, you may have to look hard for these unused phone jacks as they may be concealed behind furniture and long since forgotten. Depending on the age of the house or apartment, there may be several phone jacks within a residence. Older homes may not be wired for as many extensions as early phone service was usually only set up with one phone in the house. Additional jacks may have been wired over the years as needed. Newer homes will generally have telephone wiring in just about every room.

There are generally two types of telephone jacks; a wall-mounted jack that is similar in size and location to an electrical outlet, or a baseboard mounted jack that is made of plastic, and is slightly smaller than a deck of cards. If you dig around and find one of these unused jacks, it can be utilized to add a caller ID unit or a CID equipped telephone. Even though the cheater has deleted the data from all of the known CID units in the house, you can still secretly review all incoming calls at a convenient time.

Remember, if you use a CID phone for this purpose, be sure to turn off the ringer of the phone. The last thing you want is for your partner to hear the phone ringing under a bed in the guest room or from behind a piece of furniture. If you discover that one of these overlooked phone jacks exists in the basement, this can be an ideal place to conceal a covert caller ID unit.

You may find that all of the phone jacks in the house are in use. If this is the case, don't despair. There is an easy solution to the problem. Although a telephone will usually be visible and readily accessible, the phone jack that it is attached to will often times be hidden. You can purchase a *splitter* that can be plugged into the jack, but allows you to connect two separate units instead of one. The existing telephone can remain in its usual location and a separate CID unit or equipped phone can be concealed elsewhere. A splitter can be easily purchased at Wal-Mart, Home Depot, or any hardware store for a couple of dollars. Installation is as simple as plugging in a telephone. No wiring is required.

If you feel that the above methods are worthwhile, but none of the existing jacks fits the criteria, you may have one additional option. If a suitable phone jack is not available, you can simply install one. Now, everyone has a different level of technical ability, so you'll have to base this decision on how handy you are and if you think you can easily accomplish this task. The last thing you want to do is to try to install an additional jack and end up with phone service that is not working. Imagine the telephone company serviceman explaining to your partner that the phone is not working because someone cut the phone line in the basement. That said, I can assure you that the installation of an additional phone jack is very simple and can be accomplished with a minimal level of skill. If you don't feel you are up to the task, you should by no means attempt it, but you may have a friend who is capable and willing to help.

I'll give you step-by-step instructions now for adding a phone jack to any phone service. Additionally, there is plenty of information available online as well as books that can be found at your local bookstore or a branch of the public library that will give you in depth instructions on telephone wiring. You should only perform work on phone lines that are in your shared residence and should also be aware that there is a big difference between an owned home as opposed to a rented one. A landlord may not appreciate you altering the phone service in his property.

First things first, you must allow a reasonable amount of time to perform the work without being detected. A reasonably handy person can usually install a new phone jack, if the wiring is accessible, in about 10 to 15 minutes. I would allow a couple of hours that you know you will be able to work in privacy just in case that you run into a problem. Secondly, do not attempt any of this work if you are not thoroughly familiar with the difference between telephone wires and electrical wiring. Telephone wires carry a low voltage in order to power the telephone and operate the ringer, but this is minimal and can only give you a very mild shock. Tampering with electrical wiring, on the other hand, is extremely dangerous as they carry enough voltage to do serious harm, and can even cause death. You can see what telephone wiring looks like by opening up any phone jack in your home with a screwdriver. You will see several small gauge and very brightly colored wires within the phone jack. These smaller colorful wires will be encased in a cream colored or gray outer sheathing.

Before you begin, you will have to be sure that you have the proper tools needed for the job. You should have a flat head as well as a phillips head screwdriver, wire cutters and a wire stripper or some other way of stripping the insulation off of wires. A razor blade may also come in handy for this and other parts of the installation. You'll also have to purchase a phone jack. I would recommend a surface mount, baseboard phone jack with a modular plug. This can be purchased at any home improvement store or in the telephone department of Wal-Mart or a similar type of store.

The best place to add an additional jack is in an unfinished basement or attic as the phone wiring is usually easily accessible. In these locations, the first thing you will need to do is to locate some phone wiring. Once again, if you are not sure if the wires are for the telephone service or are electrical wires, do not attempt this procedure. There are many other ways that we can go about catching the cheater.

Once you locate a usable phone line you must also make certain there is enough slack in the line to add a jack. You can cut the line and peel back the outer casing to expose the smaller colored wires. Although they have begun to change the color-coding of these wires, most residential telephone wiring still has the original colored pairs. In a basic phone wire you will see four wires. They are green, red, black, and orange (sometimes yellow). They are used in pairs, with the green and red for line 1 and the black and orange for a secondary line if one exists. Because of the significance of the colors during certain holidays, they are often referred to as the "Christmas pair" and the "Halloween pair". In the majority of cases, we will concern ourselves with the first line or Christmas pair as this is usually the only phone line in use in the house. If there is a secondary line, and that is the line that you wish to monitor, only then will you concern yourself with the Halloween pair.

Once you have exposed the colored wires from inside the outer casing, you will need to strip the two pairs down to bare copper wire for about a quarter of an inch. Do this on both sides of the cut. You should have stripped two green, two red, two black, and two orange wires. Be sure not to touch the bare copper wire or allow them to touch each other as there can be a slight shock from the low-voltage current running through them.

With your screwdriver, remove the cover of the new phone jack. You will see four silver screws with wires attached to each. The colors of these wires should match the color of the wires in the phone line. With your screwdriver, slightly loosen the screw with the green wires attached to it. Now attach the two green wires from the phone line to the screw. You can make it this easier to do by bending the stripped copper end of the wire over the tip of the screwdriver, therefore making a hook out of the wire that you can hook around the base of the screw. Once you have attached both green wires to the corresponding screw, gently tighten down the screw. Repeat this process for each of the other colored wires. Remember not to allow any of the bare copper wires to touch each other except for those of the same color.

All that is left is to reattach the cover of the phone jack by tightening the cover screw. The jack can be mounted by screwing it to a wall or by using a piece of double-sided tape, but it is not necessary. You can test your new phone jack by plugging any working telephone into the jack. Use a non-cordless phone for this as a cordless phone will also require you to plug the unit into an electrical outlet. Be sure to check all of the other existing phones in the house to ensure that they are working properly as well.

Once your new covert jack is working, you can attach whatever you like to it. A simple caller ID unit or a caller ID equipped phone will keep a clandestine record of all incoming calls to that number. Once again, if you use a phone, make sure that the ringer is turned off. Be sure that the new device is thoroughly concealed in an out-of-the-way location to be certain that it will not be accidentally discovered. If you have kids in your house, be extra diligent in your efforts to hide the unit, as they may be more likely to happen upon it than your husband is.

Pam & Jerry

Pam and Jerry had been married for 8 1/2 years and seemed to have it all. They married right after college, and the two of them couldn't be happier. Jerry went to work as a sales rep for large pharmaceutical company and Pam taught the second grade at Thomas Jefferson Elementary. By the time they reached their second anniversary, the couple happily announced that they were expecting their first child. Pam was ecstatic and Jerry quietly hoped that his first born would be a son.

With a baby on the way, the next logical step was to move from their cramped, two-bedroom apartment in the city to a home of their own. Pam was worried about taking on the additional expense of a mortgage, but Jerry insisted that his children would have a backyard to play in and enjoy the kind of childhood that he never had.

Jerry, an only child, was the product of a broken home. His parents divorced shortly before his sixth birthday. His father was rarely present in his life and did little to help Jerry's mom financially. The two lived in a series of small and meagerly appointed apartments with several extended stays at Jerry's Aunt Mary's house scattered in between. Perhaps that's what first drew him to Pam, the promise of stability and a normal home life. He always envied Pam's family and the closeness that they all shared, wishing that he had enjoyed the kind of upbringing that she and her two sisters so fondly recounted.

Pam's sister worked as a receptionist for a local title company and referred the couple to a top-notch realtor in the area. Six weeks before the birth of baby Sarah, Pam and Jerry closed on a modest three-bedroom, Tudor style home in the Minneapolis suburb of Maple Grove. The house needed work, but the price was right. Jerry went on a tear, spending all of his nights and weekends cleaning, painting, and getting the house in shape. The two worked together painting and decorating the nursery in anticipation of the baby's arrival. The sonogram had long since revealed the news that Jerry's first child would not be a son, but he was thrilled at the prospect of being a father, nonetheless.

By this time last year, the once meticulously kept Tudor home was showing signs of neglect. Jerry was home less and less since taking on a night job at The Home Depot. Pam wasn't happy to see him do it, but she had left her teaching position shortly after the birth of their second daughter, Betsy. They tried living on one income for a while, but after the first year it became apparent that it simply would not be enough.

Pam had begun to get used to spending most of her time as the only adult in the house. She loved her kids, but it was becoming increasingly difficult conversing only with children. She would eagerly await Jerry's return every evening, but he would usually be tired and not very talkative. As time went on, Jerry became more and more distant, and even during his time at home, his mind seemed to be elsewhere.

Although Jerry's part time job was a financial necessity, Pam was becoming increasingly agitated by it. It was bad enough that Jerry was rarely around and often didn't get home until his kids were fast asleep, but the scheduling practices at The Home Depot were so erratic that Pam could never schedule any time to herself. He would constantly get phone calls at the last minute, asking him to come in to work. Jerry never refused the extra shifts, and always was quick to point out that he would not have to do this if Pam was still teaching. She began to question whether the extra $11.50 an hour was really worth the added strain on their relationship. There had to be a better way.

About six weeks ago, on a Saturday afternoon, Pam was trying to catch up on some yard work and turnover the front beds. After all, between the two jobs, Jerry was working constantly and was always too tired to chip in with the chores. The kids were watching TV and had the volume turned way up, so Jerry probably didn't hear the back door when Pam came in to grab a bottle of water out of the fridge. As she approached the kitchen, she could hear Jerry talking in a rather hushed tone. She couldn't make out much of the conversation over the blaring TV, but she could've sworn she heard Jerry say the words "I miss you too".

Jerry seemed startled when Pam walked into the kitchen and quickly ended the phone conversation by saying "okay I have to go now, I'll be there". Pam's mind was spinning, as she was yet unable to process what she thought she had just heard. All she was able to blurt out was an awkward "who was that?". Jerry explained that it was his manager at The Home Depot, and that he would be going in for inventory tonight.

For the next two weeks, Pam kept running through the events of that Saturday afternoon in her head. She never questioned Jerry any further about the phone call, but couldn't help wondering. She did begin to question herself and wondered if she had simply misheard what Jerry had said on the phone. She ran through an endless list of alternate expressions that he may have actually said, but kept coming back to the same thing; "I miss you too".

The one thing that she could not get out of her mind was the way that he seemed to rapidly press buttons on the cordless phone as he was walking out of the room. The only thing that she could think of was that he was trying to clear information from the caller ID service. Maybe she was just being overly suspicious, and after all, Jerry was working fewer shifts at The Home Depot lately and things seemed to be a little bit better. He was even helping out more around the house.

Finally, after countless sleepless nights, Pam decided that she simply had to know the truth. *A friend* explained how to add a hidden caller ID unit within the house. After all, based on the suspicious phone call, it seemed to be a good place to start. Pam knew just the spot. There was a phone jack in the nursery. That was completely hidden by a changing table. She remembered masking it off when they first painted the nursery for Sarah. She stopped by the mall the next day and purchased an inexpensive cordless phone with caller ID. She knew there was also an electrical outlet behind the changing table, so plugging in the base unit would not be a problem. By using a cordless handset, she would be able to keep it hidden somewhere else where she could easily access it without disturbing the baby. Everyday, while Jerry was at work, she would recharge the phone on the base unit.

She began to monitor the covert caller ID information on a regular basis. She did this for the next week or so, without noticing anything out of the ordinary. Maybe she was just being paranoid. In fact, it seemed the more that she paid attention to the call activity, the less phone calls were coming in. Even The Home Depot had stopped calling to ask Jerry to work extra shifts.

One evening after dinner, Pam decided to run to the supermarket to pick up a few things. Jerry was home that night so she would not have to take the kids with her and would be able to make it back in time for *Desperate Housewives*. She decided to take the caller ID handset with her and tucked it away in her bag. She laughed about it to herself on the drive to the market as she realized that the phone was well out of range of the base unit, and she would not be able to pick up any data.

It had begun to rain when Pam pulled the minivan back into the driveway. She sat behind the wheel for a few minutes with the cordless phone in her hand, wondering if she should disconnect it and try to forget about her suspicions. She really had begun to feel guilty about what she was doing. She tried scrolling through the caller ID information and quickly saw that there was no new data. With that, she wondered if the signal would reach the driveway from the base unit in the nursery. She hesitated for a moment, and then pressed the talk button. She expected to hear a dial tone when she pressed the receiver to her ear, but there was nothing but silence. She heard the voice only a split second before she was about to hang-up. She held her breath and listened silently as Jerry spoke with Gail, one of the cashiers from the Home Depot...

*69 and Other Phone Company Features

All telephone companies offer a variety of standard as well as premium features to their subscribers. Although phone companies differ as to what services are available, most in the US are similar. To see what types of services may be available from your phone company, look at the beginning of your local telephone directory in the *customer guide* to see a complete list of available features. You may be familiar with some of them and may be surprised by others.

Some of these services will be included with basic telephone service, while others will have a per use charge or require a subscription to that particular service. You should keep that in mind if your partner is the one who usually sees or pays the phone bill. Below is a list of the most common features, often referred to within the telephone industry as *Vertical Service Codes*. I have listed the ones that I feel can be the most useful for our purposes.

51 Provides the subscriber with the directory number, date, and time of all unanswered incoming calls. This is a code and feature that many people are unaware of as it is not common in many areas. If it is available, it can yield a tremendous amount of information.

57 Initiates a customer-originated trace. This will trace the last incoming call, regardless of whether caller ID information was blocked or not. You will not be provided with the caller's information, but the call will be flagged. If you're receiving harassing anonymous phone calls, this is a good feature to use. If three calls from the same phone number are flagged by dialing *57, law-enforcement can be notified and they will have access to the caller's identity.

67 Will block the caller ID data of an outgoing call. If you or your partner receive calls that say "blocked call" or "private call", the caller is likely dialing *67 before dialing. You can use this feature to anonymously call back numbers that appear on caller ID to see who answers or who the call came from.

69 This is a very popular feature and one that many people use regularly if they do not have caller ID. The service will dial the number of the last incoming call, but in most service areas an electronic voice will tell you the number of the last call before asking if you would like to dial it.

72 Will activate call forwarding. After dialing *72, you can follow the voice prompts and enter the number where you would like incoming calls to be forwarded to. Some services will forward the call immediately, while others will only be forwarded after a preset number of rings. Obviously, there are countless ways that you could use this feature to your advantage if you believe that your partner is receiving calls from another woman. Use your imagination.

73 Will deactivate call forwarding and return the service to normal operation. By only using this feature selectively, you can use call forwarding only during times that you feel are likely to yield evidence.

958 This feature may not be as common or available as it once was. By dialing 958 from a landline phone, a digital voice would read back the phone number of that phone. This was only useful if you did not know the phone number registered to a particular telephone.

Using a Pen Register

Thus far, we have spent a lot of time focusing on how to ascertain the number of incoming phone calls. Another important aspect of phone usage that we should not overlook is that of outgoing phone calls. Your partner may be hesitant to call the other woman from the home phone if it is a long distance call, but may not be quite so cautious if the number is local and unlikely to appear on the monthly phone bill.

One way to obtain the telephone numbers that have been dialed from a particular phone or from the phone service within the house is to utilize what is known as a *pen register*. This device is also commonly known as a *call register*. When you hear the cops or the feds referring to putting a "trap" on someone's phone line in your favorite crime drama, this is usually what they are referring to. A pen register will record all of the numbers dialed from a particular phone line. In the old days, they actually printed out the numbers on a registertape-like roll of paper. Today's units will record the data electronically, and that data will either be available on a display screen similar to a caller ID unit, or be able to be connected to your computer by way of a USB cable. Obviously, the value of such information in investigative terms is considerable and should not be overlooked.

A pen register will generally record all numbers dialed on a phone, not just the phone number. For this reason, it is hypothetically possible to obtain passwords and other numbers that were entered, such as voicemail pass codes. Just a little food for thought.

14

Scanners

There was a time that using a standard police scanner was a very easy way to monitor phone conversations that took place on a cordless telephone. A typical cordless or wireless phone has a base unit that is plugged into a hardwired phone line. The unit requires additional current to operate as well as to charge the cordless handset and therefore must be plugged into an AC outlet. The base unit transmits a signal through the air to the wireless receiver so that the user can move about freely while talking on the phone. It is this signal that is transmitted through the airwaves that is vulnerable to interception.

During the 1980s, when cordless phones first became popular, the units were very basic and technologically unsophisticated. The early models usually operated on one or two channels and in a frequency range of 43 to 44 MHz (Megahertz). As cordless telephones evolved, the early models soon became 10 channel and 25 channel units and were designed to operate at a considerably higher frequency. This was done as the manufacturers attempted to thwart the eavesdropping efforts of amateur radio *enthusiasts.*

The newest units operate at up to 5.8 GHz and out of range of a standard scanner's range of reception.

101

Scanners that can be used to eavesdrop on high frequency wireless telephone conversations have been banned in most jurisdictions and are very difficult to find. The scanners that you can find at RadioShack or similar type store will be of no use in monitoring modern cordless phones. You may, however, be able to find a scanner that will pick up the higher frequency telephones online or through a spy store that specializes in surveillance equipment.

In general, I don't recommend using a scanner in an attempt to catch a cheater, as there is a good chance that you'll be violating any one of numerous state or federal laws. Additionally, the type of scanner that you would need to purchase is quite expensive, and there is no guarantee that it would work for your purposes.

Step Up to the Microphone

Up until this point, we have primarily discussed how to monitor telephone activity and/or telephone conversations. There is a big difference, both legally and ethically, between monitoring a phone call and recording a phone call. As I have mentioned earlier, there is also a vast difference between what you do regarding your own phone service within your own home, as opposed to tampering with someone else's phone service in their home.

One of the easiest and least obtrusive methods of recording a telephone conversation is to use a proximity recorder in the area that the phone call is likely to take place. Now keep in mind, this approach will only be able to document one side of the conversation. In other words, you will be able to hear what your partner is saying on the phone, but not what is said by the person on the other end of the line. Even with those limitations, an intimate conversation recorded with a carefully concealed tape recorder can yield all of the evidence that you will need. Although you will be hearing only one side of the conversation, there are certain statements that are beyond reasonable explanation, regardless of who else is on the phone or what they may be saying in response.

A recording device appropriate for your needs can be easily and inexpensively purchased at RadioShack or the electronics department of Target or Wal-Mart. This type of recorder can be digital or require a tape. It can use a standard size tape or a mini cassette. The mini cassette recorders are generally smaller and easier to conceal. These type of recorders are designed for dictation and other non-investigative tasks, so you must be sure that it has certain features critical to your needs before purchasing it or putting it to use.

The first feature, you should look for is a VOX switch. This stands for *voice operated exchange* or *voice operated switch* and simply means that the microphone is voice activated. The device will only begin to record when it "hears" a sound or voice, and will subsequently cease to record once the sounds have stopped. This is important so that the machine will only record when necessary, otherwise you could find a tape filled with nothing but silence. One problem that you may run into is that the VOX switch does not differentiate between sounds and therefore could record hours of audio from a football game as your partner lays on the couch watching ESPN. There is no way to avoid this, but let's remember that this is a low-tech approach.

You must also ensure that the recorder to be used works silently. If it beeps, buzzes or clicks during normal operation it will alert the cheater. Test out the unit and see how it functions. Some units will make a loud clicking sound as the record button is released when it reaches the end of the tape. If the performance does not fit the bill, you can return the recorder and pick up another one.

The next thing to consider is the location that the recording device will be placed. Most importantly, you will want to locate it somewhere that it will not be inadvertently discovered. If you're efforts to record an incriminating phone conversation fail, you can always try again. But if your recorder is found by your partner, the jig will most certainly be up.

Try to conceal the unit in an area near where a phone conversation is likely to take place. Since many people have cordless phones in their home, a person may carry on a phone conversation in a different area of the house from that where the base unit of the phone is plugged in. Some people will move about the house doing other things while they talk on the phone. But that's okay, recording only part of a phone conversation can still provide a great deal of insight as to your husbands' or partners' activities. You have probably seen him carry on a phone conversation in the past, so you should have a good idea of where he is likely to be while on the phone. If you do not live together, you may try asking him where he is the next time you speak to him on the phone for an extended period of time. Usually there will be a favorite chair or a sofa wear a man will park himself while talking on the phone. Try to locate the proximity recorder within three to six feet of that location. If you think there may be more than one spot where he is likely to carry on a phone conversation from, perhaps you could hide the recorder somewhere in between.

Either way, once you have selected a location and put the recorder in place, turn it on and test it to make sure it records properly. Sit or stand where you think your partner is likely to be, and talk in a normal voice. If the results are not acceptable, you can try another location. Once you have settled on the final placement of the recorder, turn the power on and put it in place. Be sure that the unit has fresh batteries in it and that the tape counter, if it has one, is set to zero.

That way, you can always tell if the unit has recorded anything with a quick look at the counter rather than having to play the tape.

As to where to hide the recorder, you will notice that you have a variety of options once you begin to look for them. Choose a spot that will not likely be in the subject's line of sight when he is sitting or standing. In other words, down low, or up high works the best. Place the recorder on top of a high piece of furniture, such as an entertainment center, armoire or on a shelf that is well above eye level. You can also secure it underneath a table or other piece of furniture. Velcro or two-sided tape works best for this, but you must be certain that whatever you use will hold up over time and not allow the recorder to fall off and be discovered. For this reason, I prefer Velcro over tape, as it does not lose its sticking power over time and is not adversely affected by temperature or humidity.

Keep in mind that the uses for a proximity recorder are limited only by your imagination. You could position one under the dashboard of his car to record any cell phone calls he makes while driving. You could also monitor conversations between him and the other woman. You could record him talking about the other woman with a friend as they carpool to work. I knew of one person who actually hid a proximity recorder in her husbands satchel where it recorded a conversation containing some rather incriminating evidence. So be creative.

Recording
Telephone Conversations

The next method that we will discuss involves recording telephone conversations directly over the telephone line. Of course this is a serious step that you should consider carefully, as we are now talking about a much more advanced form of electronic surveillance.

Telephone line or recorders are readily available and can be purchased online or at RadioShack for $100 or less. Basically, these units are standard cassette tape recorders with a few basic modifications. Like the proximity recorders they will be VOX operated, but will also provide a modular phone jack on the back of the unit so that a phone line can be plugged directly into the recorder.

Another valuable feature that you should look for is a slower recording speed. This will turn the cassette tape at a slower speed and allow you to record many times longer on a standard cassette, sometimes up to several hours. Many units have a switch that will give you a choice between standard recording and extended recording. Remember, with the VOX control you will only be recording conversations, so there will be no dead space on the tape.

One other feature that is an absolute necessity is an on/off switch for the recorder's *beep-tone*. Many recorders will make a beeping sound every 5 seconds or so to alert the person on the line that they are being recorded. You have to be able to disable this feature for your efforts to remain covert.

You will have to use a modular phone wire to connect the recorder to a phone jack. You will usually have the option of running the recorder on batteries or by plugging it into a wall outlet. It is definitely better not to have to worry about batteries running out but that may be your only option if there is not a concealed electrical receptacle in the appropriate location. You should locate the telephone recorder in a hidden or out of the way place using the same guidelines that we discussed regarding covert caller ID units.

Answering Machines
and Voicemail

Most people who have hardwired telephone service within their home, will usually incorporate some type of device or service to record incoming messages. If you are married or otherwise cohabitate with your partner, the likelihood of the other woman leaving a message on the home answering machine is unlikely. If you and your partner do not live together, there is a chance that you could retrieve incriminating information from his answering machine.

If you have access to his home or apartment, retrieving this data may be as simple as making an unannounced visit to his home while he is out. This is only practical if you have a key or know where a hidden key is located. I don't want to see any of you breaking and entering your partner's residence, as this is a serious criminal offense.

If you don't have a key, or you don't feel comfortable entering his home without his knowledge, you could always leave something there accidentally during your next visit. In that way, you can call him while he is at work or otherwise not at home, and make arrangements to gain access. If it is urgent that you retrieve the forgotten item, he may tell you to stop by his office and pick up a key or tell you the location of a hideaway key.

Once you are able to spend a few minutes with his answering machine, there are a couple of things that you can do. The most obvious is to listen to any messages on the machine. If any suspicious messages exist, take note of any critical information. You should also utilize the caller ID or *69 in an attempt to ascertain the name and/or number of the caller. If there are no useful messages on the answering machine, you still have other options.

If the device in question uses a cassette tape, you may be able to access old messages that he is unaware even exist. It will help to know in advance what type of answering machine is currently in use. Older models will incorporate a cassette tape or a mini cassette to record incoming messages. Newer models are digital and do not require a cassette. For cassette models, you will have to bring a standard or mini tape player with you that can play back the answering machine tape. Before removing the cassette tape, take note of which side is facing up so that you can return it properly when you are done. If the answering machine uses standard cassettes, you may be able to play it back in the home stereo system, if it is so equipped. Be sure to take a listen to both sides of the tape as it may have been flipped over in the machine at some point. Before jumping to any conclusions, keep in mind that messages recorded on the flip side of the cassette may be quite old and not be as incriminating as they may initially sound.

Each time that a person plays back his or her messages on their cassette style answering machine, the unit will automatically reset itself and cue the tape to the proper spot, so that new incoming messages will be recorded over previous ones. When the messages are played back, the machine automatically knows to only play back the current messages. When you play back an answering machine tape in a different tape player, it does not have such capabilities and will therefore play the tape in its entirety. Because the new messages are recorded over older ones, there may be portions of longer messages still remaining on the tape.

Have you ever rushed to answer your phone only to find that your answering machine had picked up just a few seconds before? I know this has happened to me, and it has probably happened to you on occasion. We all know what happens in this case, our answering machine will end up recording either all or a large portion of our conversation. Because this "message" is substantially longer than most typical messages, it will usually still exist on the cassette tape except for the first minute or two that has been recorded over.

Once you have finished listening to any retrievable messages, be sure to return the cassette to its original location in the answering machine. Make sure you insert it with the same side facing up as when you began. Turn the machine off and then on again so that it will reset itself. If you're not sure how to do this, try unplugging the machine for a few seconds and then plugging it back in.

If the answering machine in question does not use a cassette tape of any kind, there are considerably fewer options for retrieving and reviewing past messages. Of course current messages will still be readily accessible. Examine the unit carefully as it may have a feature that allows you to listen to previous messages if they have not been manually deleted.

Regardless of the type of answering system in use, most will usually incorporate some type of method for the owner to retrieve his or her messages. This is usually accomplished by way of a *remote access code*. You're probably familiar with this feature and may use it on your own answering machine or voicemail. Generally, you will be required to dial a three or four digit code when you call in to your machine. The answering machine will then play back current messages over the phone. There may also be voice prompts or additional codes to access other features.

If you were to discover the remote access code of your partners answering machine, you would certainly have unlimited access to his phone messages. You could call his home at times that you knew he was not there and remotely listen to the messages. Remember to dial *67 to block your caller ID information as a precaution, regardless of whether or not he subscribes to the caller ID service. If something seems amiss with his answering machine, he could always dial *69 to discover who had called.

On many machines, especially the slightly older models, the access code is printed on a sticker somewhere on the answering machine itself. It can be located on the bottom or back of the unit, or sometimes on the inside cover where you access the cassette tape. Even some digital models will still have the remote access code printed somewhere on the machine. If you cannot locate the code in this way, it can often be found in the owner's manual if you should have access to it.

There is another opportunity available to capture the remote access code. Your partner may call to check his messages from your home phone or cell phone. His home phone number as well as any other digits that were dialed will be recorded on your phone. Most phones now have a redial feature. If you were to hit redial after he had made the call, his phone number as well as the access code should be displayed on the phones digital display if it is so equipped. A pen register attached to your phone line would also record any numbers that were dialed. If you were to hook up a telephone line recorder to your own phone line, you could be able to record not only the messages that he retrieved, but also the *sound* of his remote access code being dialed. Each number on a telephone keypad has a different tone. With a little practice, you can easily decipher the numbers. I can tell what phone number was dialed on a phone if I am standing close enough to hear the tones. On a cell phone, you would simply need to access your call history to see the numbers that had been previously dialed.

Your partner may not have a physical answering machine unit. He may use a voicemail service provided by the telephone company instead. If this is the case, you will not be able to use many of the tactics we have discussed earlier regarding retrieving and reviewing messages from an answering machine. The only way to access voicemail messages is remotely, and with a code. Therefore, all of the previously discussed methods for ascertaining someone's remote access code can be used just as effectively for voicemail.

Cellular Telephones

These days, cell phones have become a much more common method of communication than landline telephones. The portability and ease of use of today's cellular phones has caused many people to abandon their home telephone service altogether. Whether or not your partner solely uses a cell phone, or uses it in addition to his hard-wired service, we should certainly not overlook this valuable source of information. Even if a cheater incorporates both types of phone service, the cell phone offers greater privacy and may be his first choice for communication with the other woman.

The best way to retrieve information from your partner's cell phone is to have physical access to the phone itself. Of course, you'll have to look for an opportunity that will allow you to access it and to do so secretly. Although getting a look at a cheater's cell phone may be a much more difficult task than examining his home phone, it can also provide considerably more information about his phone usage. A cell phone will generally keep a record of all incoming and outgoing phone calls, as well as incoming and outgoing text messages. The cellular service itself will usually include voicemail service. Access to voicemail can often be done from the cell phone with the touch of a button, without entering any type of access code. You can however, usually access a cell phone's voicemail from another phone by way of a remote access code. You can use many of the same methods described in the previous chapter regarding answering machines and voicemail for trying to discover the remote access code for the cheater's cell phone.

If you are unfamiliar with the features of your partner's cell phone, you may be able to put your hands on the original owner's manual to better understand how that particular model operates. If it is not available, note the make and model number of the phone as you may be able to find operating instructions online by visiting the manufacturer's website.

There is one important difference between cell phones and landline phones that you must keep in mind. While the caller ID data available on a home phone is provided by the telephone company, the identifying information found on a cell phone is determined by the user. If a name and number shows up on your home caller ID unit, you will know that the name that appears is that of the registered owner of that phone number according to telephone company records. On a cell phone, you can program whatever name you would like to associate with a particular number. You may store a number as "Barbara-Work" or "Jim-Home". For this reason, you must be suspicious of all information collected from a cellular phone.

The first feature to check on the cell phone is the *phonebook*. This will have a listing of names of all commonly used phone numbers. Be sure to check and cross check the names and numbers in the phone book. Even the most careless cheater will probably assign some sort of code name to the other woman. In my experience, he will usually use the most innocent name he can come up with. If it is a person's name, it will most always be male. He will often times use a known friends name but add an alternate location such as "Jim-Office". You can cross check published landline phone numbers, using the reverse lookup feature of an online service such as www.whitepages.com. There are also online services available that advertise that they can provide information on cellular phone numbers as well. This service is offered for a fee. If you are unable to verify a phone number by these or other basic means, you could always call the number in question to see who answers. Be sure to use *67 to conceal your caller ID information.

Similar methods may be used when reviewing numbers in the outgoing call history. If an entry appears as a name, this means that the corresponding phone number is listed in the cell phone's phonebook. If only the actual number appears with no name, this means that the number is not listed in the phone book feature. Some cautious cheaters will not add the other woman's information to the phonebook, even under a fictitious name. Check all numbers that have been called and verify their owners.

Another area of interest to look at while you're at it is the text messaging feature. Once you locate and access the text messaging main menu, you should see options to view the message inbox, as well as the outbox. The actual text of both incoming and outgoing messages will be recorded in these two locations, respectively. Keep in mind that text messages will only be stored for a limited period of time. It may be for as long as a month, or as short as a few days, depending on the settings. Text messages can also be manually deleted from the inbox or outbox if the cheater is diligent about covering his tracks.

All of the data that we have discussed above can be accessed by using the cell phone itself, but it is also accessible by using a different method. You could opt to purchase an electronic device called a SIM card reader. SIM card readers have become increasingly easy to purchase and usually cost between $25 and $150 at your local or online spy store.

All of the information on many modern cellular telephones is stored on what is known as the SIM card. SIM stands for *subscriber identity module.* This very small card is made of plastic and is located inside the cell phone. You can access the SIM card by removing the back cover of the phone and taking out the battery. It should be clearly visible. Once removed, the card can be inserted into the reader to capture the information that is stored on it. The reader can then be plugged into the USB port of any computer to access the data.

19

Computers

Computers have become an integral part of all aspects of our human existence. We use them to work, to play, to shop, to communicate, and for our own entertainment. You don't have to look back all that far to a time when computers were more likely to be seen in a science fiction movie than in an average person's home. Most people have computers, and most use them on a daily basis. With the invention of the Internet, the average amount of hours spent per day on the computer has skyrocketed.

It makes perfect sense that you can tell a great deal about a person by their computer usage. We can learn what their interests are and who their friends are. If you know where to look, a computer can tell you what websites a user has visited, as well as who they have communicated with. Obviously, when it comes to investigating your partner's fidelity, the information contained on his computer can be invaluable.

With computer use at an all time high, and millions of people surfing the Internet at any given time, computers have become an element of just about every aspect of our lives. This includes cheating. Many illicit relationships have begun on the Internet as people "meet" and interact in cyberspace. Many would-be cheaters find this virtual world a safer, and far less intimidating environment to test the waters of infidelity. Many cyber affairs that began online continue in that fashion, with the two parties never actually meeting in person. Other individuals, who have met through more traditional avenues, will use the Internet as a means of communicating with each other. Using e-mail, instant messengers, and chat rooms can often times be a more clandestine alternative to a phone call.

There are endless types of computers, browsers and Internet service providers available to the consumer in today's marketplace. The computer portion of this text will be limited to generalities for that reason. There are, however, several places to look for information on a computer that are common to all. The investigative methods that you use will depend greatly on what type of computer system you are exploring. Play around with it a little. Computers have become very user friendly and for the most part, self-explanatory. With a little imagination and some experimentation, you should be able to uncover a substantial amount of evidence, if it exists.

As with most of the information presented in this book, you as the reader will have to determine if it is practical or ethical to utilize any or all of the following tactics. Once again, the specific circumstances of your own relationship will dictate how you may or may not proceed. If you are married to your partner, a computer may be considered common property and therefore would belong to both of you equally. Even if you're not married, but cohabitate with your partner, you may share a computer within the home. Of course, if none of these circumstances apply, certain privacy issues and legalities could arise as a result of your actions.

Tonya & Phil

Tonya had been seeing Phil since early last spring and all things considered, their relationship was good. They always had a good time together, and the sex was great. The couple first met on a Friday night at the Blue Martini, a local Orlando area hotspot. Tonya was with her two best friends in the world, Jill and Courtney. Phil was supposed to meet some friends who bailed out on him at the last minute, so rather than sit home on a Friday night, he decided to go out alone.

Phil was charming and handsome, and all of Tonya's friends loved him. They would often tell her what a catch he was and how lucky she was to land a guy like Phil. Although he slept over three or four nights a week, they still maintained their separate apartments. Phil always said that it was one of the reasons that their relationship worked so well. After all, neither one of them was looking to get married and they had no interest in having children. Marriage is just a piece of paper, and why complicate things, right? I mean, everyone they knew who was married was either divorced or seriously unhappy. So things were fine just the way they were, but still, Tonya always had a certain uneasiness about Phil. Maybe it was her own insecurity, after seven months together she should be able to trust him.

Phil was in sales and worked for a large company selling copiers and office machines. The money was okay, but the job was just temporary. Phil always had something else in the works. He was always working on an idea for an Internet startup, or working on some other idea to make money. Just last month he attended a free seminar on how to trade currency on the foreign exchange. Phil always had an angle, and it was just a matter of time before he hit it big. If all else failed, he had been sporadically writing a movie manuscript over the past three years and just knew that when it was finished, it would sell.

Tonya worked as a waitress at TGI Friday's near the Mall. She had been there for about eight months and was finally starting to get the prime stations and better shifts so that she could really start to make some good money. Before that, she had worked in the shoe department at Macy's. It wasn't a bad job, but the money wasn't great either. When Jill got hired by Friday's, she kept telling Tonya about how much more money she was making. After a year and a half of selling shoes, Tonya was ready for a change and was quickly hired after Jill put in a good word for her. The work environment was good, and she got along well with her coworkers. One of them, Jim, was recently promoted to assistant manager, which would give her an ally when it came to scheduling requests and time off.

If there was a drawback to the Friday's job, it was the schedule. By now, she had enough seniority, and with Jim filling out the schedules she could work day shifts most of the time. The only problem was that you made considerably less money working lunch. The dinner shift was always more profitable, and she really couldn't afford to pass on the extra income. So for now she would have to continue to work nights, even though it meant spending less time with Phil.

Although the opportunity to go out was limited by their conflicting schedules, Tonya and Phil made the most of their time together. Many times Phil would come over after Tonya got off work at the restaurant and spend the night. They would always go out to dinner or for drinks, and sometimes catch a movie on Tonya's nights off. Sometimes they would still go back to the Blue Martini to dance and hang out. Even though they didn't go there too often anymore, the bartenders always seemed to remember Phil. That's just the kind of personable guy that he was.

On the nights that Tonya was off from work, she would usually stay over at Phil's place after they went out. One Saturday morning after a night on the town, Tonya, awoke to the smell of fresh coffee brewing in the kitchen. Phil generally wasn't an early riser if he didn't have to go into the office in the morning, so she was rather surprised to find him up and out of bed before her. She lay there for a while, drifting in and out of sleep, running through the errands that she would have to do before work, in her mind. After about a half-hour, she started to wonder where Phil was. She hadn't heard a sound from the other room, and could see from there that the bathroom was dark.

When she finally made her way to the kitchen, Tonya realized why Phil had gotten up before her. It was 11:20 a.m.! "I never sleep this late" she thought, but concluded that she must be overtired and needed the rest. A Post-it note stuck to the coffee machine explained Phil's absence. "Went to the gym with Tommy, didn't want to wake you. See you in a bit XO me."

Tonya poured herself a cup of coffee, milk and two sugars, and plopped herself down on the couch. She would have to get a move on if she was going to make it to the bank and get her nails done before work. She didn't have to be in until four, so it wouldn't be a problem. She sat in silence for a few minutes, planning out her day when the fan kicked on in Phil's computer, startling her out of her trance. The PC sat on a tiny little computer desk in the corner of the cluttered living room. It was usually turned off when Tonya was there, and she wondered if she would be able to check her e-mail from there.

With a click of the mouse, the computer came to life as the Yahoo home page illuminated the screen. Both Tonya and Phil used Yahoo for their e-mail so she should be able to logon to her account fairly easily. In the upper right-hand corner of the screen, she couldn't help but notice the Yahoo messenger window asking if she would like to sign in. She didn't know that Phil used messenger, but the username was the same as his e-mail; *PRB1981*. The six digit password was remembered on the computer as she could see the neat row of asterisks in the password spot.

She knew she was being nosy, but the temptation to click the sign in button was just too great. After all, Phil had nothing to hide. And what did she think she was going to find anyway. The debate only went on in her mind for a few seconds. Convinced that she was doing nothing wrong and that Phil wouldn't care anyway, she signed into Yahoo messenger as Phil. Within a few seconds, a list of contacts appeared on the screen. The first thing Tonya noticed was just how many contacts there were. The list was long. She scrolled down and counted 23 different people that Phil had apparently been communicating with. The screen names themselves didn't offer much in the way of identifying the contact.   They had names like *racey7683* and *luv2laf79*. Tonya laughed to herself as she saw that one of Phil's contacts was *bucsfan999*. That had to be Phil's brother Steve, a rabid Tampa Bay Buccaneers fan.

The smile was still lingering on her lips when the sound of an incoming message nearly catapulted her off of the chair. The messenger window stared at her from the center of the computer screen. Tonya's eyes widened as the last remnants of her smile disappeared from her face. The message was from *Christy729* and simply said. "Hey where u been?" She sat there for a moment, feeling somehow caught in the act of snooping on Phil's computer. Her face felt flushed as she timidly answered *Christy's* inquiry.

PRB1981:	I've been around
Christy729:	yeah me too, haven't been out much lately
PRB1981:	so what's up?
Christy729:	I want to see you, is she working tonight?

What Have We Here?

Let's begin by taking a look to see what you can find on your partner's computer. Many people store information on their computer that they once stored as a hardcopy. Documents, letters and photographs are all commonly kept in digital format on a computer's hard drive. We can start by taking a look at the document folder for any incriminating information. Within that folder, you may find a subfolder entitled "my pictures". Although rather obvious and not likely to bear fruit, this folder is always worth a look.

While we are looking for folders on the computer, we should keep in mind that it is possible to *hide* certain items from another's view. On a Windows operating system, click the start menu and then click *control panel*. From there, you can click *appearance and themes*, and then click *folder options*. Once the *folder options* window opens, click on the tab marked *view*. A short way down the list of the *advanced settings*, you will see the following items;

- **Do not show hidden files or folders**
- **Show hidden files or folders**

One of these two items will be selected. If the second option is checked, all files and folders on the computer are visible. If the first option has been checked, this is an indication that certain files or folders are hidden from view. By selecting *show hidden files or folders*, you will make all items visible. Now return to your search and check the documents folder, the *my pictures* folder, and any other items that appear to be of interest. After your search is complete, be sure to return the computer to its original settings.

Another source of information that we will want to explore is the browser's *history folder*. This should contain information documenting all websites that have been visited by any user of the computer. Keep in mind that the browser may not differentiate between users. You would not want to wrongly accuse your husband of an indiscretion, only to discover that your teenage son had been surfing in areas that he shouldn't have been.

Now, all browsers are different and will offer different ways to access this information. You should begin by opening the browser itself. You should be able to find an icon on the desktop or on the start menu. Once you have opened the browser, look for anything marked *history*, especially on the toolbar at the top of your screen. If you are unable to locate access to the history folder, you can always click on help and search the keyword *history*.

Once you have accessed the browser's history folder, you can scroll down the list of websites that have been visited to see if anything suspicious stands out. Internet companies take great care in choosing the titles of their websites to achieve the maximum marketing value. Therefore, the content of the website will usually be blatantly apparent in the web address. You should be on the lookout for any websites that refer to dating, "hooking up", love, or have any type of sexual theme. You may discover that your partner has been viewing pornographic websites. This is a problem in and of itself, but does not necessarily indicate infidelity. You should also keep in mind that a cautious and computer savvy cheater can easily set his computer to delete the history file each time that he logs off.

Internet Chat Rooms

Another type of website that you should keep an eye out for is chat rooms that your husband or boyfriend may be frequenting. An Internet chat room is a website where individuals can sign in and engage in a group discussion. Many of these sites will offer an option for two people to move to a private chat room after the initial contact, if they should so desire. Chat rooms are a common method for cheaters to seek out new potential partners. Many chat rooms will have a theme such as singles, sports, teens or specific topics. Some are actually geared towards encouraging extramarital affairs. Visiting a chat room is not necessarily an incriminating activity. You should take into account what type of chat rooms your partner has been frequenting.

If you do discover unacceptable chat rooms listed in the history folder, you can take further steps to gather evidence. When you enter a chat room, each person will have a screen name that will appear next to all of the comments that they make. It is often the same screen name of their e-mail address. It can also be their login name for the Internet service that they are using. If you know your partner's screen name, or are able to find it out, that will be of considerable use.

Use the information contained in the history folder, as well as your partner's computer usage in general, to try to determine when he is visiting the chat room in question. You could then visit the chat room from your own computer or from another location to see if you spot him there. In this way, you will be able to read what he is saying to others. Be sure to create an alternate screen name that will not be easily recognizable to your partner, as it will appear on the chat room display once you have signed in.

Instant Messenger

Another method of communicating in real time on the Internet is by using an instant messenger service. There are countless providers of free messenger services available on the Internet. MSN, Yahoo, and AOL Messenger, just to name a few. Two parties can type information onto the instant messenger window, and both can view it and therefore carry on a conversation.

You may or may not be aware that your partner uses an instant messenger service. Using IM should not be considered suspicious behavior by any means. The best way to ascertain if he is using instant messenger to communicate with another woman is to view his contacts list.

First things first, we must determine if he has an instant messenger program running on his computer. Look for an icon on his desktop or on the toolbar if one is visible. If you cannot locate a messenger there, click on *all programs* after opening the start menu. Keep in mind that more than one instant messenger may be installed on the computer.

Once you have located an instant messenger program, click on it to open. At this point, the messenger may do a variety of things, depending on the type of service and the way that your partner has set it up. In some cases, by opening the messenger it will automatically log in to the service. Some will open a logon screen that will prompt you to sign in to the messenger. A password will always be required to logon to instant messenger, but your partner may have opted to have the computer *remember* the password so that he does not have to type it in each time he logs on. If this is the case, you can simply log into his instant messenger service.

If you are able to gain access to the instant messenger, you should be able to view contact information of people that he has communicated with. Click on the drop down menus at the top of the messenger window to see what functions are available and what information you may be able to access. There should be an address book or contact list for you to explore. Once you are viewing this list, use your mouse to select different IM contacts to see information about that particular person. Some users will create a profile, and that should be viewable at this point. Some profiles may even include a photograph. Don't assume that a contact is innocent simply by the screen name listed. Cheaters can be very clever in disguising the name of the other woman. You should investigate any unfamiliar contact names as well as the ones that sound inherently suspicious.

E-Mail

One other obvious location to search for evidence on your partner's computer is in e-mail. There are a variety of e-mail services available, many of which are free. For this reason, it is very convenient for a person to have multiple e-mail addresses for different uses. I personally have several, as I use one for personal correspondence and others for business purposes. Do not limit your search to e-mail addresses or services that you are aware of. Your partner may have established a covert secondary e-mail address solely for the purpose of corresponding with another woman.

All e-mail service providers will function differently, but there should be certain aspects that are common to all. The first area to explore is the address book. This should contain e-mail addresses of all Internet e-mail contacts. Many e-mail programs have an *auto add feature* that will automatically add the corresponding e-mail address of any incoming or out going e-mail to the address book. For this reason, a cheater may be unaware that the other woman's contact information has been added to his address book.

As always, be on the lookout for any unfamiliar names or e-mail addresses, keeping in mind that the information may be disguised. In most e-mail address books, you'll be able to click on the entry to see additional contact information.

Another interesting feature of e-mail that may be overlooked by a cheater is called *auto complete.* This feature will save the user time when composing outgoing e-mail. This is done by automatically filling in the rest of the e-mail address after one or more letters have been typed in. To explore this option, click on *compose mail* while in the e-mail program. A blank e-mail should appear on your screen. Move the cursor to the *send to:* area of the e-mail as if to enter the recipient's e-mail address. Start by typing in the letter *A*. If the *auto complete* feature is available, a list of all known e-mail addresses that begin with the letter *A* will appear. Some of these addresses will not be located in the address book. Continue the process by entering *B* then *C* and so on, until you have completed the alphabet. If no e-mail addresses appear after you have entered several different letters, the e-mail program probably doesn't have an auto complete option.

Once you have thoroughly searched for any questionable e-mail addresses, you can move on and begin to look for actual e-mails. All e-mail services will either have a mailbox or an inbox where you can access mail. Once you open the mailbox, you should have options to view new mail, old mail, sent mail, and recently deleted mail. Check each of these locations for any suspicious e-mail. There will usually be a search option included as well. Enter any questionable e-mail addresses in the search window to quickly discover any correspondence sent to or received from that address.

Most computers will also have a *personal filing cabinet* that may store copies of incoming and outgoing e-mail. Look for this option as it may contain overlooked evidence. If you should have any problems navigating through the e-mail program, simply click the help tab to find instructions on how to access the desired information.

Keyloggers and Other High-Tech Solutions

If you have used the methods described in the previous chapters to no avail, you may step up your investigative efforts by using one of the following more advanced methods. Keep in mind that the reason you may have been unable to locate any evidence by way of the more basic methods is simply because there is no evidence to be found. If, however, you feel that it is worthwhile to look further into your partner's computer usage, you may proceed as follows.

One tactic that you may incorporate is to install a surveillance program onto the computer in question. This type of program has gained popularity and is widely used by parents to monitor their children's online activities. For that reason, these programs have become readily available and can be purchased at many retail outlets, usually for $100 or less. You may also search online to view a wider variety of products.

These programs, once installed, will silently and secretly monitor computer activity and usage. Depending on the particular program, you can review hours and duration of time spent online, instant messenger conversations, websites visited as well as monitoring incoming and outgoing e-mail. To sum it up, the program will automatically collect all of the information that we have discussed in the previous computer chapters.

While computer surveillance programs can offer a software solution to your information needs, there is also a hardware solution. A keylogger is a device that is physically attached to a computer for the purpose of gathering information. The unit will record every keystroke that is entered into a computer's keyboard. It can be very useful for obtaining password data from a particular computer.

The device can be installed on a desktop PC on the cord connecting the keyboard to the computer. The unit is small, but completely visible and therefore should only be used on desktop computers, where there is an opportunity to conceal it from view. It is not practical for use on laptop computers or computers with wireless keyboards.

The unit can be left to secretly gather information and be retrieved at a later time. It can then be attached to another computer to review the recorded information. A Keylogger can be purchased online as well as from most reputable spy stores. The cost for this type of unit is between $35 and $150.

Physical Surveillance

Up until now, we have primarily discussed investigative techniques that have involved either hearing or reading incriminating evidence. While these methods for gathering information are extremely useful, the highest degree of proof can only be obtained by witnessing the illicit activity actually taking place. This can only be accomplished by conducting some sort of physical surveillance on your partner. Now that does not mean that you need to catch him in bed with another woman or anything quite so dramatic. Seeing him in a bar or restaurant with her or observing him entering her apartment would be a fairly high level of proof.

Unless the affair is categorized as a "cyber affair", and only takes place online, the relationship must involve the two parties meeting face-to-face. Some of you may conclude that you have already discovered enough evidence by using the previous methods, while others will feel the need to take your investigative efforts one step further. If you feel uncertain or if you're the type to second-guess yourself, you may need to take that additional step so that you can know once and for all if he is innocent or guilty.

Some women may feel the need to literally catch their partner "in the act" and confront him in a situation where there will be no way that he could possibly explain it away. The television program *cheaters*, has taken this approach to ridiculous lengths as they film unfaithful partners being literally caught in the act of cheating. If you have ever seen this program, it may convince you to think twice about this type of approach, as the confrontations often get out of hand, and in some cases even become violent.

You may not be looking to confront your husband or boyfriend right there, on the spot. Perhaps you are just looking for that ultimate level of certainty before confronting him at a later time. Every person requires a different level of proof to feel absolutely certain that he is or isn't cheating. The objective of this book from the start was to provide you with conclusive proof, either way. You must now decide if you have reached that point or if you need to take it one step further.

Physical surveillance can be accomplished by using one of three possible methods. The first and most obvious method available to us is the *eyewitness approach*. You must put yourself in a position to see for yourself with your own eyes what type of activity is taking place. This *catch him in the act* approach will leave little doubt in your mind as to what your partner has been up to.

The second method is basically a variation of the first, and is known as the *secondhand eyewitness*. In other words, you will allow someone else to witness the activity in question and report back to you. This approach can work well if the cheater is in a place where you would easily be spotted yourself. The best example of this is to send an accomplice into a bar or restaurant where you know your partner is. Of course, you should only enlist the help of a friend who will not be recognized by him.

The last of the three methods involves using what I call a *remote eyewitness.* This involves recording the activities of your partner without his knowledge, so that you can view video documentation at a later time and draw the appropriate conclusions. This approach will require you to use some type of video equipment to record the illicit activity.

If you live with your partner, the odds are considerably less that he will carry on an affair in your own house or apartment. He is much more likely to meet the other woman at her home or some other location. That said, I have seen cases where a husband and his mistress conducted a long-term physical relationship in the marital home, right under the nose of the man's wife. If you do not cohabitate with your partner, the odds are greater that an affair is happening at his home. Either way, you should have gathered enough information at this point to have some insight as to where you think the illicit activity is taking place.

If you believe that the affair is taking place in your shared home or at his place, the first thing that you will want to do is provide him with an opportunity to meet with the other woman. You can use whatever fictitious circumstances you like and are sure that he will not question. Try to create the opportunity at a time that coincides with any patterns you have observed in the past. Make sure that you plan on being unavailable for a considerable amount of time as he is not likely to arrange a rendezvous if he thinks you will only be occupied for an hour or so. You can physically watch the apartment or house to see who is coming or going. Take note of vehicle information such as make, model, color, and license plate number as this could be useful at a later point. You may want to swap cars with a friend to make sure that you won't be spotted. If you are sure that both your partner and the other woman are inside the home, you could always make a surprise visit and catch them in the act.

If the prospect of sitting in a parked car for a couple of hours or endlessly driving around the block doesn't appeal to you, you may want to consider the remote eyewitness approach. In the chapter on computers, we discussed software that is designed for parents to monitor their children's computer usage and how we can use it for our own purposes. Similarly, *Nanny- Cams* have become a popular way for parents to keep an eye on their kid's nannies and babysitters to ensure their children's well-being. They can also be used in our investigative efforts.

These compact and easily concealed camera units have become increasingly affordable and easy to purchase. They can be bought at RadioShack or at any reputable spy store for about $150. The camera should be concealed in an area that it will not be discovered and in a place where illicit activity is likely to take place. Use the same guidelines that we incorporated to hide a recording device. You are not looking to record cinema quality footage here, only too clearly and accurately document what is going on. A cleverly concealed camera placed low to the floor usually works best. Some cameras are incorporated into everyday household items so that they do not have to be concealed.

If you don't feel that the affair is taking place within the home, you'll have to take additional steps to discover the location. In the next chapter, we'll discuss how to do just that. So get ready, we're goin' mobile.

Vehicle Surveillance

Ninety percent of all affairs will involve traveling by car to meet the other woman. "Tailing" your partner's car can be a very effective method of ascertaining his whereabouts and activities. If you are considering following him, there are certain guidelines that you must follow to ensure that your surveillance efforts are effective and go undetected.

The first and most important rule of any vehicle surveillance operation is safety. I cannot stress this enough. You must exercise extreme caution and obey the appropriate traffic laws at all times. There are no exceptions to this rule. Your safety, as well as the safety of pedestrians and other drivers is considerably more important than losing the subject in traffic. Aside from the obvious safety concerns, you would not want to receive a costly traffic ticket for a moving violation. It is not uncommon for even the most experienced investigator to lose their subject during the course of a mobile surveillance. You must keep things in perspective. While doing this type of surveillance, it is very easy to get caught up in the moment and feel a certain sense of urgency. While this is common, it is definitely not warranted. Try to remain calm and relaxed. If you lose him today, you can tail him again tomorrow.

When conducting a mobile surveillance, you should have someone else do the driving if at all possible. In that way, the person operating the vehicle is not as emotionally involved in the situation and will be less likely to act in a rash manner. It also allows you, as the passenger, to focus your attention on observing the subject vehicle. You can give the driver instructions as to where to turn and so on. It also gives you the opportunity to duck down and out of sight if you should find yourself in a precarious position where you might otherwise be detected. As I have mentioned previously, it can be extremely valuable to have a trusted friend to assist you in your efforts.

Another important measure is to use a vehicle other than your own. If you have enlisted the help of a friend as suggested above, you could use his or her car for the surveillance. Even the most careless cheater will have some level of awareness when he is up to no good. Your car will stand out like a sore thumb, especially if he is in route to meet the other woman. If you absolutely have no one available to assist you and do the driving, at the very least you should swap cars with someone else so that you will be less likely to be recognized. You may even consider renting a car if you feel the expense is justified.

The ideal time to conduct any type of vehicle surveillance is in the evening, after dark. This usually works out well, as more often than not, illicit activity takes place during the nighttime hours. It is much more difficult to spot a tail in the dark than it is during the daylight hours. In the daytime, a vehicle's make, model, and color, as well as the driver's identity, are all clearly visible, even at a distance. At nighttime, a vehicle is only visible by its lights, and a driver is less likely to notice if the same vehicle has been behind him for any length of time. If you have disregarded my previous suggestions about using an alternate vehicle, you should only attempt to tail your partner at night to ensure that you are not spotted.

Before you begin to follow your husband or boyfriend's vehicle, there are some things that you should do in advance that will assist you in your efforts. The first thing that you should do is write down the license plate number of the subject vehicle. This may seem like an obvious step, but it is often overlooked. Many people are unable to recall their own license plate number, no less that of their husband or boyfriend's vehicle. At this time, make note of any bumper stickers or damage to the back of the vehicle that will help you to spot it in traffic.

You should also take a good look at the back of his vehicle and memorize the configuration of the taillights, brake lights, and turn signals. It will be helpful if you have the opportunity to spend a few minutes alone with his car, and especially beneficial if you can do so at night. Turn the vehicle's lights on and stand back 30 to 50 feet away. This will give you a clear image of what the vehicle will look like when you are tailing it and help you to avoid losing sight of it. You can also turn on the turn signal to see what it looks like when blinking, or have an accomplice depress the brake pedal to see the brake lights operate. If you'd really like to be thorough, take a photograph of the back of the car.

In the old days, it was not unheard of for a private detective to break a subject's taillight to make it easier to follow the vehicle from a distance at night. Now I am not suggesting that you do damage to anyone's car. That just wouldn't be right. However... the same result can be achieved if you have access to the trunk of the vehicle. Some vehicles have easier access to the taillight housing than others. If it is accessible, you may be able to loosen one of the taillight bulbs so that it will not work. This can usually be accomplished by pushing in on the bulb itself and turning it one-quarter turn, counterclockwise. Keep in mind that the driver of the vehicle may be subject to a traffic ticket or fine if he is pulled over by the police.

Now that you have taken some preliminary measures, you must decide when and where you will conduct the vehicle surveillance. By using the evidence that you have gathered already, and reviewing the information that you have recorded in your journal, you should have a good idea as to when would be a good time to follow your partner. You can narrow down the time based on his past patterns of behavior. To increase your odds of success, you may want to create an opportunity for him by telling him that you have to work late or some other set of fictitious circumstances.

Every vehicle surveillance must have a starting point. You must decide where you will begin "tailing" your partner. The most common point of origin is his home or place of work. You should plan to arrive well before his expected departure and keep some distance between you and his vehicle. If his car is parked in a parking lot at work, with only one exit, you would want to set up in a location where you could observe the exit and not necessarily his vehicle. The same can be said for a residence. There may only be one likely route from his home out to the main thoroughfare. Therefore, you would be less likely to be spotted if you waited to intercept him out on the main road as opposed to parking right on the street where he lives.

Once he departs, take note of the time, and the direction that he is traveling. The most common mistake made when tailing a vehicle involves determining how far back to follow. If you're too close, you may be spotted, and if you're too far back, you may lose the subject in traffic. So use your own judgment. A general rule to follow is that you must stay closer to a vehicle during city driving as traffic lights and other vehicles are more likely to interfere. When traveling on the highway or in a more rural location, you can keep a greater distance between yourself and the subject vehicle. As I mentioned earlier, tailing a vehicle at night will allow you to stay closer without being observed.

As drivers, we are trained to watch what is happening in front of us and to anticipate what is likely to occur. We are very aware of the upcoming traffic lights and vehicles that are trying to pull out onto the roadway. When following another vehicle, the driver must remain aware of these things, but also anticipate what is likely to happen in front of the subject vehicle as well.

The most common way to lose sight of your subject's vehicle is by getting stuck at a traffic light. If your partner's car is approaching a green traffic signal and you are some distance back, you may want to accelerate a bit to ensure that you will make it through the light as well. This may close the gap between the two vehicles, but you can drop back to an appropriate distance once you have passed through the light. If he makes it through the light and you have to stop, don't panic. Although the seconds will feel like minutes as you wait for the light to change, be patient. The cycle of most traffic signals is only 45 seconds to one minute long. You will have plenty of time to re-establish contact with the subject vehicle.

The most common reaction to getting stuck at a traffic light during a surveillance, is to literally *floor it* once the light turns green. Although you should try to catch up to the subject vehicle, do not overreact. This can result in overshooting your target. I have seen cases where an overzealous investigator raced to catch up with the subject vehicle, only to find himself stopped at the next traffic signal and sitting directly next to the target. Always remember the golden rule; safety first. If you lose him, you can always pick up his trail further down the road or at another date and time.

If you successfully follow your partner to his destination, there are a couple of things you must keep in mind once he gets there. As you are probably unaware as to where he is going, his journey is likely to end rather unexpectedly, as he pulls into a restaurant parking lot or stops in front of a home or apartment building. Your first reaction will be to stop the car immediately and park somewhere so that you will be able to observe him when he leaves the vehicle. At this point, you are at a very critical stage of the surveillance and you should not do anything to draw attention to yourself or your vehicle. In most cases, the best thing that you can do is to drive on by so that you will not be spotted. If you have to pass in close proximity to your partner's vehicle, duck down in the passenger seat while your driver continues on. If he was at all aware that he was being tailed, he will take a good hard look at the following vehicle when he gets out of his car. Continue on down the street or around the corner. You can circle back and find an appropriate location to park and observe. Don't take too much time to do this as your partner may just be stopping off somewhere for a moment before continuing on to his final destination. He may be picking up the other woman to go out to dinner or to some other location.

Take note of the address and any other information that you observe about the location. If it is a residence, take down the make, model, color, and license plate number, of any vehicles parked there. If your partner's destination is residential, you can access state or county public records or any one of many online services to ascertain who lives at that address.

In most of the previous chapters, I have tried to provide you with simple techniques for gathering information, followed by more advanced and high-tech solutions. This chapter will be no different. I'm sure you have seen detectives electronically tracking a vehicle in the movies or while watching your favorite crime drama on television. While this technology was once extremely expensive and not readily available to the general public, that is no longer the case. The advent of GPS, or *Global Positioning Systems,* has made it possible for anyone to utilize this technology for their own purposes. As I write this book, the new iPhone was just introduced and incorporates GPS technology into every handheld unit.

Electronic GPS vehicle transponders can be purchased for under $200 either online or at any reputable spy store. These compact and relatively inexpensive devices can be concealed underneath a vehicle, under a seat, or in the trunk. They usually have a magnet on the back for quick and easy installation. The basic units will internally record the location of the vehicle for future review. You will not be able to monitor your partner's location in real time, as is done on TV, but you will have a record of where the vehicle has traveled to once you retrieve the transponder. Most units can be connected to any computer by way of the USB port so that the data can be easily uploaded.

Debbie & Mike

She had tried just about everything. She had monitored his phone calls, she dug through his computer, and she searched his car. And yet, she still couldn't find any proof that he was being unfaithful. Maybe she was just being paranoid, but no matter how hard she tried to ignore the feeling she had in the pit of her stomach, it just wouldn't go away. It was hard to put into words exactly what it was that was different about him, but deep down inside, Debbie new that Mike was cheating. It was an all too familiar feeling, and it was really starting to take its toll on her. She even spent a rather unpleasant hour digging through the trash. She didn't expect to find much of anything there. After all, that was how she caught him the last time, and she didn't think he would make the same mistake twice.

They had been married for six years and it had been almost three since Mike's last misstep. At least as far as she knew. They had been going through a rough patch, and Mike was under a lot of pressure at work. She didn't notice at the time all of the obvious signs that Mike was displaying. Debbie knew that she had been naïve the first time around, and she was not about to be played for a fool again.

It was really embarrassing to think back to the last time, when she first found out that Mike was having an affair with one of the girls from work. Any fool could have seen what was going on, it was that apparent to everyone. At least that's what they said after the fact. None of Debbie's friends ever told her at the time that they thought Mike was cheating. They were just afraid to bring it up. It was only later that they all admitted having their doubts about him. Her friends were very supportive though, through it all, none more so than Cheryl.

Debbie and Cheryl had been friendly since college, but really didn't know each other too well until the incident with Mike three years ago. Cheryl was good friends with Nan, one of Debbie's best friends from high school, and that's how they first became friends. Cheryl was great in a crisis. She was always the one you could count on when the chips were down. The voice of reason. When Debbie was at her lowest, it was Cheryl who stepped up and was always there for her. So in a strange way, Mike's affair had been the catalyst for them becoming such close friends.

So now, when she needed a friend the most, it was Cheryl sitting behind the wheel as they waited for Mike to leave work. The two sat silently in Cheryl's Honda and both wondered to themselves how the evening would end. Mike had said that he was going out with his friends after work, a habit that was becoming more and more common of late. It was early December, and already dark by six o'clock, making it easier for the pair to go unnoticed as they sat just down the street from the Ford dealership where Mike worked. He had been a service advisor there since being promoted last year from the repair shop. It was a nice bump in pay, and it was nice to see him with clean fingernails for a change.

It was about 6:15 p.m. when Debbie first spotted Mike's black pick-up pull out of the lot and head east on Fremont. "THERE!" she said, pointing through the windshield. They had set up about a half block west of the dealership, as they felt pretty sure Mike would head east into town and wouldn't likely pass them. Debbie's heart rate quickened ever so slightly as Cheryl started the engine and eased the Accord out into traffic. Mike's F-150 pick-up did not have any real distinguishing characteristics when you looked at it from the rear, and Ford pick-ups were everywhere in the east Texas town of Longview. There were a lot of cars on the road and they were able to stay pretty close without fear of being noticed. Cheryl followed about two cars back, and one lane over.

If Mike was really going out with his friends from work, they would probably all be headed over to Hurley's. It was the only place in town that you could still find a lively crowd on a weeknight. It was ladies night at Lasso's, but the service crew certainly wouldn't be dressed appropriately after spending a full day under the hood. Hurley's was a favorite spot for happy hour, and when Mike turned left onto Ridgecrest, Debbie felt sure that he was headed there.

Maybe she was being overly paranoid. Maybe he was just having a few beers with the guys. There's nothing wrong with that, right? Debbie often went out for lunch or shopping with *her* friends, why should she be uncomfortable because Mike was getting together with *his*.

Mike had been with Cafferty Ford for almost 8 years now, and some of his best friends were his coworkers. He really worried if things would change after he got promoted, especially since Doug and Carl had been passed over for the service advisor position. At first it seemed a little odd, but everyone seemed to make the adjustment pretty quickly. After the first couple of weeks, it was business as usual, with Doug ribbing Mike about his mustache, and just about everyone picking on Carl. They were a good bunch of guys and all things considered, Debbie liked Mike's friends.

Debbie's mind was wandering as she pictured Mike and the boys shooting pool and whooping it up around the pool table. She was almost smiling when Cheryl broke the silence. "Well, he's not going to Hurley's." Cheryl said in a disgusted tone. Debbie's eyes shot up from the floor mat to see Mike's truck continuing on past the bar, without slowing down a bit. Her eyes widened and she suddenly felt sick to her stomach. She racked her brain trying to think where he might be headed at this end of town, but for the life of her, she couldn't come up with a single possibility. They would just have to continue on and see where Mike would lead them.

The two stayed pretty quiet as they tailed Mike's pickup out of town and on to the interstate. There were quite a few cars on the road at this time of the evening, but Cheryl still kept a good distance between the Accord and the F-150, just to be safe. While Cheryl kept her focus intently on the taillights up ahead, Debbie just sat there in a state of disbelief.

They only stayed on the highway for about 20 minutes before the turn signal on Mike's truck alerted them that he was taking the next exit. Debbie had passed the exit for Hallsville on the countless trips to see her mom, but had never been to the town or known anyone who lived there. Mike made a right at the end of the exit ramp, and then turned left at the next intersection. After four more turns, Cheryl felt certain that she would never be able to find her way back to the interstate in the dark.

When the black F-150 turned into the driveway at 1764 Leland Avenue, Cheryl drove on by and tried not to look conspicuous. "Scooch down" she urged, and Debbie silently slid down in the seat. By the time they turned around at the next intersection about a quarter mile down the road, Debbie was sobbing. Cheryl kept her left hand on the wheel and her right on Debbie's shoulder as they crept back down the road towards number 1764.

Mike was nowhere to be seen, and although the inside of the house was well lit, she could not see anything from the street as the blinds were all closed. Cheryl could see that Debbie was not going to be able to do much else, so she just let her be as she turned off her car's headlights and coasted to a stop just next door to the small ranch house. Mike's truck was in the driveway and parked behind another car that looked like a white sedan. Cheryl got a pen and a piece of scrap paper out of the glove box, and did her best to get out of the car without making a sound.

When she returned a couple of minutes later, she handed the crumpled piece of paper to Debbie and quickly started the car. She waited till she was a few hundred feet down the road before turning the headlights on and finally exhaling. Debbie had begun to compose herself and held the paper up close to her face so she could see it in the dim light. On it, it said; "white Buick LeSabre" and noted the license plate directly below it. Cheryl had also scrawled "1764 Leland" on the paper.

The two didn't say much as the Honda Accord sped away from the ranch house at 1764 Leland Avenue. They weren't quite sure what the future would hold for Debbie and Mike. There were still a lot of questions that needed answering. Neither of them knew who lived in the house and drove the white Buick, but Cheryl knew one thing for sure. They were going to find out.

How to Become a
Human Lie Detector

Have you ever thought; wouldn't it be nice to always know when someone is telling you the truth or if they are lying to you? Imagine what a valuable skill that would be. You could use it in business, friendships, and romantic relationships, not to mention the edge it would give you at the poker table. While this may be viewed by some as a superhuman power, akin to flying or x-ray vision, it is a skill that you can learn and become proficient at in a relatively short period of time. Police detectives and professional investigators who spend considerable amount of time interviewing suspects have honed these skills to perfection. In the following pages, you will learn how to detect when someone is lying to you by reading a variety of their physical and verbal cues.

When we speak, there is a certain synchronization of our speech, eye movements, facial expressions, body language, and gestures. This is not a conscious process but rather happens on a subconscious level. When a person tells a lie, it throws off this synchronization, as the words do not match what the mind knows to be the truth. Do you remember as a kid, challenging someone to simultaneously rub their stomach and pat their head? It seems simple enough, but it is an extremely difficult feat to accomplish. When a person lies, it is difficult enough for them to focus on speaking the untruthful words, and near impossible for them to focus on their physical gestures at the same time.

For that same reason, a good actor will totally immerse him or herself into the mindset, emotions, and motivations of a character in order to create a believable performance. A liar does not have the luxury of reading the script in advance and rehearsing the conversation as it plays out. He probably will be mentally prepared for the first few lines of the discussion, but after that he will be forced to ad-lib, and the inconsistencies will become quite apparent.

The Eyes Have It

Have you ever seen a high stakes poker tournament on television? It can be quite interesting to watch. The first thing you will undoubtedly notice is that many of the players look more like the Unabomber than professional gamblers. Poker players know from experience that their physical "tells" can tip off their opponents if they are bluffing or not. Many will wear sunglasses to hide their eyes to ensure that they don't give anything away.

I'm sure you have heard the expression that "the eyes are the windows to the soul". As with many old adages, there is a great deal of truth to it. Eyes can show a variety of a person's feelings and emotions at any given time. You may have heard about scientific studies that address the direction that a person looks when they are lying. While much has been written on this topic, many people confuse the information and sometimes get it reversed, much like "is it feed a fever and starve a cold, or feed a cold and starve a fever". Below you will find the meanings behind each eye direction. Keep in mind that the results will be opposite for a left-handed person.

Looking up and to the left indicates that a person is accessing the *visually creative* part of the brain. If you ask someone to imagine an image that they have never seen before, they will look up and to the left as they are "visually constructing" the image.

Looking up and to the right indicates that a person is accessing the memory portion of their brain and remembering something that actually took place. If you ask a person, "what color was the first house that you lived in?", their eyes will look up and to the right as they "visually remember" the image.

Looking to the left indicates that a person is using the *auditory creative* part of the brain. If you ask someone to think of a sound that they have never heard before, they will look to their left as they try to imagine the sound. An example of this type of question would be "think of the sound that a koala bear makes" or something to that affect.

Looking to the right indicates that the person is accessing the auditory portion of their memory. If you asked that person to think of a sound that they have actually heard in the past, they will look to the right as they remember the sound. For example; "think of the sound of your grandmother's voice".

Looking down and to the left indicates that a person is accessing the *kinesthetic* part of their brain. This is the area of the brain that stores memories related to smell, feeling, or taste. If you asked a person to remember what it felt like when they graduated from college, they would generally look down and to the left as they recalled the feeling. Another example would be "think of the smell of your grandfather's pipe smoke".

Looking down and to the right indicates that a person is using the *internal dialogue* portion of the brain. This is the part of the brain that a person uses when they talk to themselves. This is true whether or not the dialogue is actually spoken or just in the person's head.

There has been much debate about the accuracy of the above information, but over the years and through countless interviews, I have found this technique to be accurate more often than not. Beyond these accessing clues, there is a great deal more information that you can ascertain by watching a person's eyes during the course of a conversation.

There are a countless number of expressions that can be made with the eyes, all having different meanings. When we speak of the eyes, we should also include the eyebrows in our observations. For example, widening of the eyes or raising of the eyebrows can be a sign of shock or disbelief. All indicators should be taken within the context of the conversation. Look for expressions in the eyes that do not match the words that the person is speaking.

Glassiness or watery eyes are often a sign of nervousness and can indicate discomfort. While we have all seen a child's eyes begin to well up with tears when they are caught in an uncomfortable situation, this trait can still be true in adults to a much more subtle extent. When a person's eyes water, even slightly more than is normal, it will cause them to blink more often than usual.

One of the most discussed aspects of lying as it relates to the eyes, is that of eye contact. I'm sure you have heard people say that a person will avoid eye contact when telling a lie. While this can be true in some cases, it is often the exact opposite. Many people, men especially more than women, know that eye contact is a sign of sincerity and truthfulness. While a woman will usually ovoid eye contact when telling a lie, a man will often times make an effort to keep direct eye contact with the person that he is lying to. This will often seem forced or unnatural, as the liar has to make a conscious effort and go against his own human nature.

While having a discussion with a person who is trying to conceal the truth, you will often times notice a pattern as it relates to eye contact. If a man just returned home from a night out with his friends, and is discussing it with his wife or girlfriend, he may avoid eye contact while discussing his evening in general terms. When asked a specific and pointed question, only then will he make an extra effort to make direct eye contact, to ensure that he is seen as believable.

Body Language Indicators

There are many physical movements that are key indicators of dishonesty. You may be familiar with some that are quite obvious, while others are much more subtle and difficult to detect. Remember, lying is uncomfortable to some extent for 99% of all people. Some signs of discomfort are almost always apparent in a person's body language when they are being dishonest.

When you are looking for physical clues that a person is being less than truthful, you should keep an eye out for any signs of discomfort. A liar will often feel warm, or begin to sweat when being dishonest. Perspiration on the forehead or dampness on the

163

clothing, especially under the armpits, could be a sign that a person is uncomfortable. Sweaty palms, although cliché, are also a sign of nervousness.

Watch for any flushing or blushing of the face and neck, as this can be a telltale sign that a person is uncomfortable. Some people's ears will become red when they are flushed. Some people will tug at their clothing, especially around their neck and collar when they begin to feel warm. I'm sure you have seen your partner feel uncomfortable in the past, regardless of the circumstances, therefore you should have some idea of how he acts in that type of situation.

Another much discussed sign of lying is touching the face or neck. Some liars will have a subconscious tick that they are completely unaware of, that can be easily spotted when you pay close attention. You will often notice a person touching their face, nose, or mouth while lying in an unconscious attempt to hide their mouth. Others will touch or tug at their ears as if to say "I can't believe what I'm hearing". Touching or rubbing the eyes is a convenient way to break and avoid eye contact in an uncomfortable situation.

A person can also show physical signs of lying by the way that they move or position their body. You have probably heard that a person crossing their arms in front of them is a sign that they are closed or otherwise not open to the discussion. While this has been shown to be true, there are many other body language cues that indicate dishonesty.

A person will often show the palms of their hands in an expression of openness. This gesture is a subconscious one that dates back for centuries. By crossing his arms, a person is not only displaying a closed posture, but is also doing a great job of concealing the palms of their hands. Putting your hands in your pockets is another classic way to conceal the palms. Others will try to use their hands as a barricade to block off their face, mouth and body from their inquisitor.

Many people focus on the hands when trying to determine if a person is being dishonest, but you should also take note of the position of the feet. A person who is lying will subconsciously attempt to "un-ground" himself and have as little contact between the floor and his feet as possible. A sitting person can do this easily, but someone standing can also shift their weight so that less of their feet are touching the ground.

As I mentioned earlier, the hands can be used as a barricade to give a person a feeling of protection if they feel that they are under attack. While the hands are convenient for this purpose, and always available, a liar may be able to find a better barricade amongst his surroundings. Anything can be used for this purpose as the liar tries to put something between himself and the other person. It can be as small as a coffee cup or a drinking glass, or larger like a chair or a kitchen island. Moving behind any type of an inanimate object is a subconscious effort to fend off your questions.

A person may also act fidgety or display a variety of unconscious movements while they are lying or involved in an uncomfortable conversation. Tapping a finger or a foot is a classic sign of discomfort or impatience. Look for suddenness or jerkiness to a person's movements or motions, as that is often the most telling attribute of discomfort.

Many expressions that we use in day-to-day language are based in truth. Our body language can often reflect some of those expressions. When we say, "face up to it", that is a more literal expression than figurative. When confronted, a person will often avoid directly facing his inquisitor. Be observant and take note of his stance. If he consistently turns his shoulders or body so as to not face you, he may not be "facing up" to the situation. If you notice this behavior, subtly change your location so that you are positioned directly in front of the person you are questioning. If he is being dishonest or avoiding the subject, you will notice that he will consistently shift his body to avoid facing you directly.

Another common expression is to be "taken aback". When a person is thoroughly engaged and interested in what you are saying, they will often lean in towards you. It is a sign of elevated interest. On the other hand, when a person feels defensive or wants no part of the conversation, they will often lean back as to distance themselves from you and your questions.

Clenched fists are an obvious sign of hostility and lack of openness. A person may also "hunch down" in an effort to make themselves a smaller target. In general, you should look for clusters of body language cues and movements that do not seem to coincide with the words being spoken.

Verbal Cues and Miscues

As mentioned earlier, it can be very difficult to focus on more than one thing at any given time. While this is true for a liar, as he tries to control and manipulate his words and body language, it is also a challenge for the person trying to detect his lies. During most conversations, you as the listener will focus your attention on the words being spoken. In most cases, you may be completely oblivious to a variety of other indicators. The brain is concentrating on hearing the words of the other party, and processing what those words mean and also imply. When we are suspicious as to the truthfulness of what we are being told, we are also analyzing a person's statements for consistency and accuracy. To successfully detect whether or not a person is lying, you must learn to focus not only on what is being said, but how it is being said.

In the following pages, we will look at some common speech characteristics that can often be telltale signs of lying and/or nervousness. Keep in mind that there can be many common reasons for any of these indicators. You should listen for multiple signs, as well as repeated specific indicators. When a person is lying, you'll often notice a change in a pitch or tone of their voice. A higher pitch usually indicates that the person feels defensive about what they are saying. You should not confuse a higher pitch with higher volume, as that is more a sign of aggression rather than defensiveness.

You may also notice a change in tempo or rate of speech. A person may slow down their speech when they tell a lie in order to be careful that they are choosing their words correctly. A liar may also speed up the tempo of their speech in a subconscious attempt to get the lie out as quickly as possible, as if by saying it quickly, it may go unnoticed. Now I know it sounds contradictory to say that both speeding up and slowing down the rate of speech can be a sign of lying. What we are looking for a here is a change in the person's overall speech patterns.

If you listen to anyone speak for a few minutes, you will notice that we all put emphasis on certain words throughout the course of a conversation. A single sentence can have several different implications based on what word has been emphasized. Likewise, a liar will tend to put emphasis on the words associated with denial or the words that he is trying to convince you of. Once you start to listen for the emphasis on certain words, you will begin to see a pattern.

All people have different speech patterns and liars are no exception. Some people will try to give as little information as possible when they are trying to deceive you. You'll notice that he will often respond to your questions with questions of his own when taking this minimalistic approach. For example,

Question; "where have you been?" Response; "what, you mean just now?" This type of liar will consistently try to give you as little information as possible to avoid incriminating himself. His answers will often seem vague and incomplete.

As we have seen previously, there are often contradictory types of behavior that can be evident when lying. While the liar described above will keep his answers as brief as possible, other liars will respond by giving more information than was initially asked. If you are dealing with someone who fits this profile, resist the urge to respond to their explanations immediately and just keep quiet. The liar will go on and on explaining his answers in greater and greater detail. In this situation, you can literally give him enough rope to hang himself.

While the two scenarios we just discussed are at opposite ends of the spectrum, notice that they are both to an extreme. A normal response would probably fall somewhere in between those two. Therefore, you must pay close attention to the person who is either giving way too little information or way too much.

During the course of a normal conversation, it is very easy to quickly answer questions as they are asked of you. Simply put, it is easy to tell the truth, but it takes considerably more effort to lie. When you ask a person a question that he intends to answer untruthfully, he must think on his feet and become creative when generating an answer. The mental process of recall is nearly instantaneous, while creativity is a considerably slower process.

With that in mind, it is easy to see how a dishonest individual will need to find ways to stall in order to have time to create fictitious answers to your questions. Just about anything can be used as a stalling tactic. A person may repeat the question back to you, or pretend that he did not hear you or understand the question in order to buy more time. He may also answer you with his own question, asking you to be more specific in your question. Unnatural pauses, excessive "Ums" and "Uhs", or seeming distracted by something else in the room are all methods of stalling. He may also seem to become flustered, as he struggles in his mind to come up with a viable and believable answer to your question.

Be aware of inconsistencies in his statements and over-compensation. Once you begin to listen for these cues, they will become more apparent. Using humor at an inappropriate point in the conversation is also an indicator.

Putting It All Together

Now that we have discussed how to recognize the key indicators of dishonesty, it's time to put it all together. Now I know what you're thinking, while all of the signs that we have discussed so far are quite effective, none of them can be considered an absolute indicator that a person is lying. After all, many of the indicators that I have given you include two opposites that both might indicate deceptive behavior. For example, too much information or too little information. So how then, can we use these indicators to find out if someone is lying to us?

To answer that question, we must first consider the most reliable technology available to identify and pinpoint deceptive behavior. The polygraph machine, or lie detector as it is commonly known, is a mechanical device that when used properly, can determine the truthfulness of a subject's answers to specific questions.

Although we all know the purpose of the polygraph, we need to understand how it works so that we can apply the same principles to our less sophisticated techniques.

If you have never been subjected to a polygraph examination, I will explain the process here. The subject sits upright in a chair and multiple sensors are connected to the persons fingertips, arm, and around the chest. These sensors will monitor the subject's, respiration or breathing, heart rate or pulse, blood pressure, and level of perspiration. The polygraph machine will record all of this data. When the person is first hooked up to the lie detector, the examiner will calibrate the machine to take into account that most people are understandably nervous while taking a polygraph. The examiner will then ask a series of questions, some of them true, and some of them false, and note the differences in the subjects vital signs.

While it may seem that the most important data received during the polygraph exam is the vital signs noted when a person is telling a lie, that is only half of the equation. The subject's physiological response while answering questions truthfully is equally important, if not more important, in determining his honesty. The examiner will always begin by asking questions that he knows the answer to for sure. He will then begin to intermittently ask questions where the answer is unknown. He will continue to alternate both types of questions during the course of the interview. The questions may look something like this;

"Is your name John Doe?"
"Were you born in New Jersey?"
"Is your birthday January 17th?"
"Did you murder your wife Sally?"
"Do you live at 123 Maple Street?"

By asking questions that the examiner already knows the answer to, he is able to observe the subjects vital signs during the times that he knows he is answering truthfully. This method is known as establishing a *baseline*. Once the examiner knows what constitutes normal vital signs for this particular subject, he will look for abnormalities in the results. Every person has different vital signs, therefore, a rapid heart rate or elevated blood pressure cannot be considered indications of dishonesty. That may simply be the subject's normal state. It is the abnormalities that are most indicative of the stress associated with lying.

Now that we see how important it is to have a baseline or a point of reference, you can see how this can be applied to the indicators we have discussed earlier. By first observing how a person acts when telling the truth, it will become increasingly apparent and easy to detect when they are lying. As with the polygraph examination, the abnormalities or changes in pattern, is what will pinpoint an untruthful statement.

Police detectives who regularly conduct interrogations of criminal suspects are extremely skilled at spotting patterns of behavior during the course of an interview, as well as the abnormalities associated with lying. These investigators did not acquire this ability overnight. They learned these skills with time and practice, and so can you. It may seem difficult at first to focus on behavior other than the actual words being spoken, but once you get in the habit of doing it, you will find it increasingly easy.

The best way to start is by practicing with a friend. You don't even need to tell him or her what you are doing at first. Simply observe the eye movements, hand gestures, body language, and speech patterns of your friend while they speak. After a while, you can suggest that he or she tell you five things that they did during the past week, but make up one of them. Watch your friend recount the five experiences. You have the advantage of knowing that four of them are being remembered, while one of them is being created. Try this a couple of times. You will be amazed that you can tell which story is false.

Once you get the hang of it, you can begin to look for baseline behavior in your partner. Casually ask questions about his activities and observe his responses. Stick to conversations about subjects that are innocent so that he will act calmly and naturally. Don't just ask yes or no questions, but instead ask for details that will require him to recall information. Pay close attention to his eye movements as he is remembering and relating information to you. Make a regular habit of making these observations and you will have established a baseline that you can use for comparison at a later time when you suspect that he is lying to you.

When you find yourself at a time when you believe that you are being lied to, you will have all of the skills that you need to differentiate between fact and fiction. Keep in mind that a liar will have rehearsed in his mind the basics of his story and may be able to tell them without showing any changes in pattern. The key is to ask him questions that he will not be prepared to answer. Do not take an accusational tone, but rather ask casually as if it were out of curiosity. While he may have rehearsed his answers as to where he has been or who he has been with, he will be caught off guard if you ask an unexpected question like "what did you have to eat?" or "was that same band playing there?". Now he will have to create an answer that he was certainly unable to prepare in advance. If he is telling the truth, the answer will be quick and natural. It will not require any extra effort for him respond to your questions. But if he is being deceitful, believe me, you will see a whole cluster of the indicators that we have discussed here and you will know for sure that he is lying.

Remember, a single indicator may be cause for concern, but look for multiple indicators and patterns of behavior. With a little practice, you can become a Human Lie Detector.

A Final Word

Well, we have certainly come a long way together. At the beginning of this book, I told you that you would be provided with all of the tools and techniques that you would need to conduct your own investigation as to your husband's or boyfriend's fidelity. We have covered the signs that are your first clues that something is amiss, as well as basic steps that you can take to confirm or disprove your suspicions. I have also given you a wide range of more advanced, and in some cases high tech, methods that you may choose to employ during the course of your investigation.

Over the years, I have seen countless cases, of all kinds. In some instances, men who appeared to be completely honest and faithful were later proven to be cheaters. At other times, I have seen seemingly suspicious behavior that, in the end, turned out to be completely innocent and the suspicions unwarranted. Suspicion and uncertainty can have a very damaging effect on an otherwise healthy relationship. By seeking out the truth, you will be able to eliminate that uncertainty from your mind and discover the answers to all of your questions. I do not know what the future holds for you, but I do know that whatever answers you may find, you will be better off for having found them.

You should always remember, above all else, that every person absolutely deserves honesty, loyalty and faithfulness from their partner. Cheating is always, always the fault of the cheater. Never let anyone tell you otherwise.